Adopting
the
Racing
Greyhound

Also by Cynthia A. Branigan

The Reign of the Greyhound: A Popular History of the Oldest Family of Dogs

third edition

Adopting
the
Racing
Greyhound

CYNTHIA A. BRANIGAN

HOWELL
BOOK
HOUSE

Howell Book House
Published by Wiley Publishing, Inc., New York, NY

For general information on our other products and services or to obtain technical support please contact our Customer Care Department within the U.S. at 800-762-2974, outside the U.S. at 317-572-3993 or fax 317-572-4002. For group sales call Wiley Customer Service at 800-225-5945.

Wiley also publishes its books in a variety of electronic formats. Some content that appears in print may not be available in electronic books.

Library of Congress Cataloging-in-Publication Data:
Branigan, Cynthia A.
Adopting the racing greyhound / Cynthia A. Branigan. — 3rd ed.
      p. cm.
      Includes bibliographical references and index.
      ISBN 0-7645-4086-6 (alk. paper)
      1. Racing greyhound.   2. Dog adoption.   I. Title.
      SF429.G8B73   2003
      636.753'4 — dc21
                  2003004389

Manufactured in the United States

10 9 8 7 6 5 4 3 2

Third Edition
Book design by Scott Meola
Cover design by José Almaguer
Book production by Wiley Publishing, Inc. Composition Services

This book is dedicated, with love and gratitude, to
KING (Low Key Two)
Without whose gentle spirit and inspiration
This book could not have been written.
The work continues in his name . . .

(Photo: Ann G. Krisher)

Contents

ACKNOWLEDGMENTS   viii

FOREWORD   ix

PREFACE TO THE THIRD EDITION   xi

INTRODUCTION   xiii

1	A Brief History of the Breed	1
2	Choosing the Right Dog for You	11
3	The Racing Life	41
4	In a Home	55
5	Care and Feeding	82
6	Insecticides and Anesthesia	109
7	Training	121
8	Having Fun	141

APPENDICES

I	Other Sighthounds	154
II	The Greyhound's Anatomy	160
III	Veterinary Information	161
IV	Adoption Groups	166
V	Resources and Organizations	198

INDEX   202

Acknowledgments

For their technical advice and assistance, and for their dedication to excellence in their field, the author wishes to thank the following:

John Ard, Greyhound trainer, formerly of Seabrook Greyhound Park, New Hampshire

Dr. Marc Elie, Dr. Ruth Haag, Nicole Timbrook, Veterinary Referral Centre, Little Falls, New Jersey

The Greyhound Project

Dr. Cynthia Holland, Protatek Reference Lab, Chandler, Arizona

Dr. Alan Klide, associate professor of veterinary anesthesia, University of Pennsylvania School of Veterinary Medicine

Christine Makepeace, REGAP director, Seabrook Greyhound Park, New Hampshire

Charlotte Mosner, Reynolds Greyhound Enterprises, Atlantic Beach, New York

Dick Quackenbush, owner of Hay Hill Kennels, Green Brook, New Jersey

To the loyal, hard-working volunteers of Make Peace With Animals, my sincere gratitude.

To my husband Charles Rissel, who makes it all possible, my love and appreciation.

To Dale Cunningham and Beth Adelman of Howell Book House, my thanks for their many efforts in bringing this book to its current edition.

Finally, to all of my animals who have gone to the other side, our connection lives on.

Foreword

It isn't every author of a foreword to a book who will tell you to
beware. But I am doing so. I am not saying, mind you, to beware
of the dog because this book is about one of the most endearing
breeds of dog in the world. Nor am I saying to beware of this
book — which is one of the most thorough manuals of adoption
that has ever been my pleasure to read. What I am doing, however, is saying to beware of the author.

I first met Cynthia Branigan nearly 20 years ago when she was
a newspaper reporter in Philadelphia. Since that time I have
known her as a friend and long-time fellow worker at The Fund
for Animals. I am telling you this because The Fund for Animals
specialized in the rescue of all kinds of animals — wild burros
from the Grand Canyon, wild goats from San Clemente Island,
wild horses, wild pigs and even the last Atlantic City Steel Pier
Diving Horses. I learned early on that Cynthia, who loved all animals, was also a marvelous adopter of all animals. Indeed whatever animal we rescued, Cynthia could and would find the right
person to adopt it.

I remember well the day Cynthia told me she had fallen in love
with a dog. I knew she had been working with Greyhound rescue
and had in fact set up her own society for that task — so I asked
her if the object of her affection was a Greyhound. She said it was.
His name, she said, was King. With that she poured out paean of
praise and superlatives about not only King in particular and the
entire Greyhound breed in general but also why everyone, man,
woman and child, should have one.

I am, of course, kidding to ask you to beware of this woman.
Cynthia is much too much of a professional to want anyone to
adopt an animal who is likely to be incompatible with that animal. Instead, as her book makes amply clear, she is just as interested in whether you are right for the dog you think you want to
adopt as in whether that dog is right for you.

This book goes into virtually every conceivable situation that a person adopting a Greyhound is likely to encounter. But with its completeness the book is also extraordinarily readable, including both the proud history of this oldest of all purebred dog families as well as fascinating individual stories from people across the country who have decided for humanitarian reasons, or for the simple desire for companionship, to adopt.

Don't think I'm going to let the beware idea go completely, though. It is true Cynthia leans over backward to point out the adjustments and even difficulties you may have. But somehow in between the lines of these cautions you can read clear as crystal Cynthia's deep and abiding love for these creatures. "Don't worry," she is saying, "go ahead. You will not regret it."

CLEVELAND AMORY
1992

$\mathscr{P}$reface to the $\mathscr{T}$hird Edition

When the first edition of *Adopting the Racing Greyhound* was published in 1992, there were exactly 42 Greyhound adoption groups in the United States. By the time the second edition appeared in 1998, there were 213. Now, in 2003, there are more than 250, and new groups seem to be forming every day. Even overseas there are other countries being heard from. To what can we attribute this phenomena?

As much as I would like to think that the sales of more than 100,000 copies of the previous editions of this book are responsible, I cannot claim credit. And, as knowledgeable and hardworking as the burgeoning Greyhound adoption groups are, I think that the real credit should go to the Greyhounds themselves.

Former racing dogs, once the best-kept secret in the dog world, are now becoming an increasingly common choice as a companion, and for good reason. Gone are the days when people would look in amazement to see one of these long, slender athletes outside the racing environment. Now they can be found on city sidewalks, suburban streets and country lanes. In fact, it is hard to image where they are not now seen, and under what circumstances they cannot thrive.

Of course, that is a bit of an exaggeration, and one of my goals in this third edition is to discourage people from getting a Greyhound without first giving the matter a great deal of thought. The Greyhounds, and their legion of fans, sell themselves so well that some people who should not be adopting are being tempted to do so. It is understandable why this happens: It is hard not to be attracted by the Greyhound's gentle and loving nature. The problem is, there is more to owning a dog than simply gazing into their eyes when you have the time, and all of that needs to be discussed and taken into consideration before you sign on the dotted line.

Another of my goals in this expanded edition is to provide the latest information on, and advances in, Greyhound health. Greyhounds have no more, and perhaps fewer, health issues than do other dog breeds; but they do have their idiosyncracies, and it is important that those who are unfamiliar with the breed (and this can include veterinarians) understand that what is normal for the general canine population may not be normal for a Greyhound. A prime example of this is the mistaken idea that most Greyhounds have underactive thyroids. I have also provided updates on safe new flea, tick and heartworm preventives, and even included a chart of exactly the type and amount of anesthesia your veterinarian should use for your ex-racer. All of the above is backed up by painstaking veterinary research by some of the country's leading authorities in their fields.

Finally, while reviewing the two previous editions of this book, I had the opportunity to reflect on the more than 4,000 Greyhound adoptions I have overseen personally through my organization, Make Peace With Animals. Since I adopted my first Greyhound, King, in 1987, and found a home for another in 1988, I have had the opportunity to witness firsthand both the joys and pitfalls of those many transactions. It has been my sincere attempt to share that practical experience with you, to help make your adoption as seamless as possible and to steer you away from some common, and easily avoidable, errors.

As I reread the book and looked back at the photos, I saw a younger and perhaps more idealistic self than I am now. King, who I adopted when he was 10 years old, was still vigorous in those days, while Ajax, by comparison, was not much more than a pup. Both had long, happy lives and have since gone on to the next thing. There have been several others in between: Fiona, Poppy, Imhotep, Whitney, and Buck. Currently, three Greyhounds share my heart and home: Zygmunt, Rosebud and 57 Chevy. If this book imparts even a fraction of my enthusiasm for the breed, and my gratitude for their extraordinary gentleness and companionability, I will have achieved my ultimate goal.

Introduction

When people harbor misconceptions about retired racing Greyhounds, they generally hold one of the following: that the dogs are old pensioners with at best only a year or so left of life, or that they as a breed are suited only for racing.

I'm happy to report that neither is true.

Until recently, when racing Greyhounds were finished with their careers, the fate met by many was euthanasia or sale to research laboratories. Now, thanks to the efforts of adoption centers across the country, these dogs are finally having their day.

Former racing Greyhounds are, in many important ways, unlike other dogs. Even seasoned dog owners may find some of their behavior baffling. Psychologically, physiologically and even historically, these dogs are different. Consequently, methods of training and care need to be adapted to fit their special needs. It is not that they are more difficult — quite the contrary — but they are unique. If you follow the advice in this book, all of which is based on extensive research and a good deal of personal experience, you will be able to help them fit in with ease.

Most Greyhounds available for adoption range in age from two to five years. Given that their life span is estimated at 12 to 14 years, you can well expect to have a long and happy time with your ex-racer.

Racing is both highly competitive and physically demanding. Many young dogs may seem, to you, to be faster than the speed of light. But, compared to others of their breed, they don't quite measure up. These "slow" dogs, not much more than pups, may be sidelined almost before their careers begin. Other dogs may have suffered a minor injury on the track. While it probably doesn't affect them at all as a companion, it may have been enough to slow them down. In a sport where every second counts, this, too, may be a reason for retirement. Finally, there are the dogs that had a full racing career. By the age of five, most Greyhounds — even the superstars — have run out of steam. But, again, nearly two-thirds of their life is still ahead of them, and after all their hard work they, perhaps above all others, deserve a good retirement.

Greyhounds have, for thousands of years, been bred to do two things: run like the wind and work together with other dogs. They were not bred to be solitary hunters, and the transition from hunting to racing has kept the spirit of cooperation intact. For this reason, Greyhounds tend to get along with other dogs. Yet the muzzles worn by the racers cause some to infer that they are fighters. Not so. In Greyhound racing the dog whose nose crosses the finish line first is the winner. The muzzle helps make the nose more prominent and assists the judges in determining which dog won.

Of course, there is a safety factor involved. Whenever you have eight dogs, of any breed, in hot pursuit of something, be it a ball or an artificial rabbit, their natural desire to get the prize can cause the mildest dog to become competitive. But, once the object of their desire is removed, almost like magic they become their sweet old selves again.

Greyhounds are extremely companionable, good-natured dogs. In fact, as a breed, they seem to have a higher-than-average incidence of smiling. When they are very happy, such as when you get home, or when they want to play, many raise their upper lip and show their teeth. This is accompanied by wild tail-wagging and prancing. Who among us can resist such a goofy display?

There are two types of people for whom a retired racing Greyhound is ideal: those with families and those without. Let me explain.

Greyhounds, especially young males, have a great deal of patience, and most seem to understand that small children must be handled with care. If the playing gets too rough, Greyhounds tend to walk away rather than snap. Of course, children should always be supervised when playing with any dog and must be taught to respect the animal's feelings. But, as many families can attest, Greyhounds and gentle children are perfect together.

And for singles who are looking for an affectionate, loving pet, a Greyhound can't be beat. You will be rewarded many times over for whatever attention you give your dog. Greyhounds, perhaps because of their long and aristocratic history, are "to the manor born." They thrive in a home environment and take to it as if they waited all their lives for the experience. They are the sort of dog that likes keeping you within sight and have been known to follow their "person" from room to room.

In 1930, the British dog writer James Matheson praised the retired racer as a companion. He said of him, "His intelligence defies all attempts at description. There would appear to be nothing which he does not understand either in word or in gesture or the shadow of coming events. When your favorite has done his work, cherish him and give him a place with yourself for the rest of his but too short life. It is his one drawback. He should live as long as his owner."

By choosing to share your home and life with a Greyhound, you are participating in an act nearly as old as civilization itself. These are the same dogs that slept alongside the Pharaohs, hunted with the noblemen of the Middle Ages, and have inspired artists and poets for thousands of years. Without a doubt they are worthy of us. The question is, are we worthy of them?

Chapter One

A Brief History of the Breed

*M*ost dog-care books devote a page, or at most two, to the history of the breed they are discussing. There's a very good reason for this: there isn't that much history to tell. Greyhounds, however, have been with us longer than any other purebred dog. To appreciate fully your dog of today, it is useful to see him in a historical context. What follows is a brief outline to whet your appetite. For a more detailed look at the Greyhound's long and rich history, you might enjoy another book I've written — *The Reign of the Greyhound: A Popular History of the Oldest Family of Dogs* (Howell Book House, 1997).

THE GREYHOUND FAMILY

When contemplating the history of the Greyhound, it is useful to think in terms of the Greyhound family. As much as anyone may tell you that this or that breed is the oldest known to man, the truth is no one knows for sure. What we do know, however, is that the earliest purebred dogs were of the Greyhound type. The Greyhound family has several characteristics in common. Among them are long legs, a long narrow head, a deep chest and the ability to hunt by sight (hence the term sighthound, or gazehound) rather than by scent as most dogs do. As this type of dog moved to different parts of the world, some of his superficial characteristics,

1

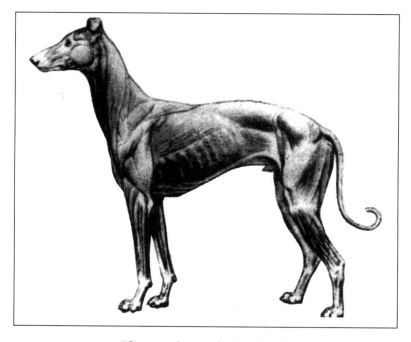

The musculature of a Greyhound.

such as the length of his coat and the shape of his ears, began to change to accommodate the conditions of his new environment.

MEMBERS OF THE FAMILY

Members of the Greyhound family that are recognized by the American Kennel Club are Afghan Hounds, Borzois, Greyhounds, Ibizan Hounds, Irish Wolfhounds, Pharaoh Hounds, Salukis, Scottish Deerhounds and Whippets. Fringe members include Basenjis and Rhodesian Ridgebacks (which hunt by sight but do not share a physical resemblance) and Italian Greyhounds (which share a physical resemblance but don't hunt at all).

THE FIRST GREYHOUND TYPES

The first traces of the long, lean dogs of the Greyhound type were seen in the ancient city of Catal-Hüyük, located in what is now southwest Turkey. Temple drawings, dating to 6000 B.C., show a hunter pursuing a stag with the help of two Greyhound types.

As people migrated to different parts of the globe, they took their dogs with them. About 4000 B.C., in what is now Iran, a funerary vase was created that was decorated with the image of Greyhounds. Obviously these dogs were held in high regard for their image to have been added to so personal an item.

ANCIENT EGYPT

It was in Egypt, however, that the Greyhound really came into his own. Not only were the dogs kept as companions (in addition to being hunting partners), but they were practically worshipped.

The Egyptian god Anubis.

The Egyptian god Anubis was, as were many Egyptian deities, half man and half beast. In this case the beast was, depending on which sources you consult, either a jackal or a Greyhound. In looking at a painting or statue of Anubis, the resemblance to the present-day Pharaoh Hound is unmistakable.

The Egyptians valued their Greyhounds so much that the birth of one was second in importance only to the birth of a human boy. Indeed, when a pet Greyhound died, the entire family would mourn by shaving their heads, fasting and wailing.

Greyhounds were mummified and buried along with their owners, and the walls of the tombs were often decorated with figures of favorite Greyhounds that had died before their owners. Among the Pharaohs who kept Greyhounds were Tutankhamen, Amenhotep II, Thutmose III and Queen Hatshepsut. Cleopatra, too, was an aficionada.

While the ancient Israelites did not worship Greyhounds and, in fact, seemed to regard dogs in general with disdain, they did make an exception for the Greyhound. It is the only breed of dog named in the Bible. Proverbs 30: 29–31 reads:

> There be three things which go well, yea,
> Which are comely in going:
> A lion, which is strongest among beasts and
> Turneth not away from any;
> A Greyhound;
> A he-goat also.

ANCIENT GREECE

When explorers from Greece traveled to Egypt, they were suitably impressed by the Greyhounds and managed to take some back with them to their homeland. The dogs' popularity caught on to such an extent that even the Greek hero Alexander the Great kept one, which he named Peritas.

The first dog mentioned in literature, in 800 B.C., was, you guessed it, a Greyhound. In the *Odyssey,* Homer told the tale of the return of Odysseus, who had been away from home for 20 years. The only one who recognized him was his Greyhound, Argus, who was only a pup when Odysseus left.

Greek mythological figures were frequently portrayed with Greyhounds. Hecate, goddess of wealth, is often shown accompanied by a Greyhound, as is Pollux, protector of the hunt. And, of course, the famous story of Actaeon and Artemis tells of the goddess taking revenge on Actaeon by turning him into a stag and setting her 48 Greyhounds on him.

ANCIENT ROME

The ancient Romans appropriated many things of value from Greek culture, and this included an appreciation of the Greyhound. Their gods and goddesses, too, had Greyhounds, and the most well-known story is of Diana, goddess of the hunt, who gave her best friend, Procris, a Greyhound named Lelaps. Lelaps accompanied a hunter into the woods and, when the dog spotted a hare, went off in hot pursuit. The gods watched the scene and, not wanting the hare to be killed, turned both it and Lelaps into stone. This scene of Lelaps chasing the hare is often depicted in Roman art.

The Romans loved to run their Greyhounds, but in even those bloodthirsty days, there was at least one person who had a vestige of humanity. In A.D. 124 Arrian wrote a treatise entitled "On Hunting Hares." He urged his readers to concentrate more on the sport and less on the gore, stating, "The true sportsman does not take out his dogs to destroy the hares, but for the sake of the course and the contest between the dogs and the hares, and is glad if the hares escape."

MEDIEVAL AND RENAISSANCE TIMES

During the Middle Ages, a time of famine and pestilence, Greyhounds very nearly became extinct. They were saved, however, by clergymen who protected them from starvation and bred them for noblemen. It was during this period that ownership of a Greyhound became the exclusive right of the nobility.

King Canute enacted a law in 1016 in England that prohibited any "meane person" from owning a Greyhound and punished any infraction severely. A hundred years earlier in Wales, King Howel decreed the punishment for killing a Greyhound was the same as for killing a person — death.

Since Greyhounds were the first breed of dog mentioned in literature, it is only fitting that they also were the first breed of dog written about in the English language. In the late fourteenth century, Geoffrey Chaucer wrote in *The Canterbury Tales,* "Greyhounds he hadde as swift as fowels in flight." Shakespeare, too, mentioned them. In *Henry V* he wrote, "I see you stand like Greyhounds in the slips, / [Straining] upon the start. The game's afoot!"

During the Renaissance, the elegant lines of the Greyhound were not overlooked by the most famous artists of the era. Among those who saw fit to immortalize these dogs in art were Veronese, Pisanello and Uccello. While Veronese's works tended toward the sacred, Pisanello and Uccello seemed to appreciate the Greyhound form for its own sake. Uccello's painting "Hunt in the Forest," for example, shows dozens of Greyhounds in a dark woods helping hunters capture their prey.

COURSING

The sport of coursing, which has its origins in ancient Greece, helped keep the Greyhound a popular animal. As coursing was originally practiced, two Greyhounds would be "slipped" (released) in a field to run after a hare that also would be released but given a 100-yard advantage. The victor was not necessarily the dog that caught the rabbit, and, in fact, quite often the rabbit escaped. Instead, the dogs were judged by a complicated set of rules that valued such things as the dog's agility and concentration. In the mid-1700s, a set of rules was developed that helped popularize the sport and caused it to spread throughout Great Britain and across the Continent.

A Greyhound head by the Italian Renaissance artist Pisanello, circa 1400.

A modern Greyhound head shows very little change.

Two famous coursing Greyhounds, Riot and David, from an 1878 engraving.

THE BULLDOG BREEDINGS

The mid-1700s were also important in Greyhound history for
another reason: it was then that an eccentric English nobleman
by the name of Lord Orford began his now-famous Greyhound-
Bulldog breedings. His idea was that by breeding a male Bulldog
with a female Greyhound, the result would be a dog that had a
uniformly smooth coat (which had eluded breeders up until that
time) and which would possess what Lord Orford called
"courage." Bear in mind, however, that the Bulldogs of those
times did not look like the Bulldogs of today. They had a much
longer muzzle and resembled Bull Terriers.

8

Lord Orford's crosses continued for seven generations, and the resulting dogs were of such high quality that those who had previously been skeptical were now clamoring to buy his dogs.

ON TO AMERICA

As people from the British Isles emigrated to America, they often brought their Greyhounds with them. Coursing was a sport that was a natural for the wide-open expanses of the prairie, and the participants justified the killing of rabbits with the argument that they were helping to protect the farmers' crops from hungry hares. General George Custer coursed his 14 Greyhounds on the day before his defeat at Little Big Horn. Perhaps he had a premonition about the next day's battle because directly after coursing his dogs, he sent them off with an officer into town so they would stay out of harm's way.

Hecate was a second-generation cross from the Bulldog breedings of Lord Orford in the mid-1700s.

Greyhound racing is a sport made in the United States.
(Photo: National Greyhound Racing Association)

GREYHOUND RACING . . . AN AMERICAN SPORT

In the early 1900s, Owen Patrick Smith invented the artificial lure that accomplished two things at once: it allowed more people to see the Greyhounds as they were raced on an oval track, and it eliminated the need to kill live rabbits. And so, Greyhound racing was born. In the years since, Greyhound racing has become increasingly popular. It reached its peak in 1991 when it was the sixth most popular spectator sport, with revenues of $3.4 billion from betting. Casino gambling has sharply cut into Greyhound racing's popularity, and profitability, but it is still a major industry. In 1995 the total betting revenue was $2.5 billion.

But the history of the Greyhound is not finished yet. The one you write with your dog will be the most interesting of all.

Chapter Two

Choosing the Right Dog for You

*A*s wonderful as dogs are in general, and Greyhounds are in particular, I consider it my responsibility to do something you might think strange: I want to discourage you from proceeding. Why? For the simple reason that, as someone who has presided over many thousands of adoptions ranging from horses and burros to Greyhounds and cats, I have come to see that some people rush into getting a pet without fully considering the long-term implications. The consequences can range from merely annoying and time-consuming for adoption workers, to tragic for the animal.

Sad to say, many people decide to get a dog for all the wrong reasons. For some it is part of a larger fantasy that revolves around a house with a picket fence and the statistical 2.2 children. For others, it is a way to stave off loneliness while they are between relationships. Some couples use a dog as a surrogate child to see how they will fare as parents of a "real" (read: human) baby. Some people who had no intention of adopting take the plunge without any forethought because they "fell in love" with an animal.

The funny thing is, you can have a dog, a house with a picket fence and 2.2 kids, and all of you can live happily ever after. Likewise, dogs can be great salves to loneliness, they can teach you a lot about responsibility, and, I can assure you, you can fall in love with them. But the difference lies in your primary motivation. It is fine to have more than one reason for acquiring a dog, as long as your main reason is wanting to provide a safe, loving home for the length of the animal's life.

Be honest with yourself: Does a dog really fit into that idealized family scene, or is he likely to become just one more chore as you are trying to juggle a job, children, housework and the million other details of life. Maybe you are lonely right now, but if Mr. or Ms. Right appears on the scene, will the dog be left behind? Finally, dogs are dogs, not children. Once your human family comes along, are you going to have time for a dog? Are you going to be willing to introduce, and supervise, the dog with the children? If you are planning to have a family, you might be better off waiting to get a dog — any dog — until the children are older and more self-reliant. As for falling in love with an animal, it seems that our feelings for dogs can parallel our feelings for people. What seems like love today can turn out to have been nothing more than a passing attraction tomorrow.

Remember, there is more to owning a dog than simply feeding him twice a day. Dogs need exercise, training, grooming, regular (often costly) veterinary care and lots of attention and affection. Can you afford all of this in terms of time and money?

SHOULD YOU BE GETTING A DOG?

Before you go any further, you need to give serious thought to whether or not you are ready for the responsibility of *any* dog. No one can predict everything in the future, but a potentially ill-fated adoption can be avoided if you simply take the time right now to think before you take on this added obligation. Please consider the following:

Is your job secure? Are you likely to be transferred? Caught up in downsizing? Try to determine which way the wind is blowing at work: Talk to your boss, ask fellow employees if they have heard anything about possible layoffs. Even if your job is secure, if you work very long hours a cat (or two!) may be a better choice.

If you rent a house or apartment, are you *positive* having a dog is allowed? If it is allowed, is there a weight limit on the size of the dog? Is the building likely to be converted to one that does not allow pets? If you are a tenant, you should ask these questions of your landlord in advance and *make sure you have it in writing.* It is also useful to have a lawyer review your lease to see what your rights are if the building comes under new ownership.

Is your marriage/relationship on solid ground? I know this is a tough question, but for the sake of the pet, it is one you must ask yourself. Adoption agencies and animal shelters are full of pets who are the unwitting victims of divorce. Many times, these animals have spent their prime years with a family and now that they are older, they are both less adoptable and less adaptable. In some cases, their reward for the many years they spent as a devoted companion will be euthanasia. By the way, adopting a dog will no more "save" your relationship than having a baby will and, if anything, will only increase the tension. Also, if you are already separated and a divorce is looming, will you be obliged to sell your house? If so, what will happen to your dog?

If you recently lost a dog, are you sure you are over the grieving process? Some people are fine getting another dog the day after their previous pet has died, while others need several weeks or months to regroup. If you know that getting another dog (particularly one of the same breed) will help you heal, then by all means, proceed. But consider the possibility that for some people it may stir up sadness that is still unresolved. Since every dog is unique, there is no such thing as replacing your deceased pet. Are you likely to compare the new dog unfavorably to the old one? Do not consider getting a new dog unless you are willing to accept him on his own terms and are willing to recognize his unique gifts. Incidentally, if you currently have a dog who is aging and/or ill, consider carefully whether or not a new addition will cause him to feel pushed aside, either literally or figuratively.

How old are you? If you are either on the younger side or the older side, I have some things for you to think about:

For those in their late teens or early twenties, you are at an age when your life can take many unexpected turns. You may decide on college, or on traveling, working on a freighter headed for distant ports or even starting a family. These can be exciting years but, assuming you take your responsibilities seriously, owning (and keeping) a dog might prevent you from pursuing your dreams. It isn't fair, and may not even be possible, to drop the dog off with your parents, and it certainly isn't fair to the dog or an adoption agency to return a dog that you acquired on a whim. Wouldn't it make more sense to wait to get a dog until you are at a more stable point in your life?

For those in their mid- to late seventies, now that you are retired, a dog can be a wonderful addition to your life. But, as difficult as it may be to face, you must consider where you will be in five or ten years time. Perhaps you will decide to move to an easier-to-maintain apartment and pets will not be allowed. Will your fixed income permit you to spend whatever will be needed on veterinary care? How is your health? Will the day-to-day care of an animal prove too taxing? Is it likely that in a few years you might have to move into an assisted living facility or nursing home?

Needless to say, if you are a senior citizen and decide to get a dog, you should not get a young one. Many pets over the age of six or seven are in excellent health, need less exercise, and are already well-versed with the ins and outs of being a good companion.

How are you fixed financially? The fee for adopting a dog is nothing compared to the lifetime of expenses you will incur. The following are estimates for the upkeep of a medium-size dog for one year:

- Annual veterinary check-up/lab fees, $60–$125

- Inoculations, $40–$75

- Prevention of internal/external parasites, $100–$150

- Food (dry kibble), $250–$500

- Miscellaneous (collar, leash, license, toys, grooming, etc.), $150–$300

All of the above, $600 to $1,150, is what you will spend in one year. Obedience training (highly recommended!) will be an additional, one-time expense of $100 to $200. Should your dog become ill, unforeseen medical expenses can add up quickly. Yes, you can prevent some illnesses, but not all. Yes, you can get pet health insurance, but it is not free, and it also has some restrictions. Do you have a fat enough wallet, or a high enough limit on your credit card, to take care of a dog properly?

WHY, SPECIFICALLY, DO YOU WANT A GREYHOUND?

If you have thought about all of the issues I've just mentioned and are as sure as you can be that you have what it takes to be a responsible dog owner, you must now think about why, of all the breeds in the world (not to mention the mixed breeds), you have decided that a Greyhound is the type of dog for you.

All of us who have adopted Greyhounds have been moved, in part, by the plight of retired racers. But if your motivation in adopting is solely because you feel sorry for the dogs, then it is possible you could serve the Greyhound cause better by volunteering with an adoption agency and helping them find other people to adopt. You might also consider making a donation to an adoption group or helping them organize a fund-raiser. You would be amazed at the expenses incurred by adoption groups, and most welcome donations enthusiastically. If you really aren't sure how to proceed and would like a dry run (no pun intended!), another possibility is to volunteer with an adoption agency to foster a Greyhound. The group will, of course, check your references and make sure you have the necessary facilities. Fostering could serve two purposes: You can see whether or not you really enjoy the Greyhound personality and you can provide a much-needed temporary home for a dog who is in-between things. Who knows — you may wind up adopting the foster dog yourself!

WHAT A GREYHOUND IS, AND ISN'T

Did you know that all purebred dogs were developed for a purpose? Very few breeds (with the notable exception of many of the toy breeds) were created to be what we call pets. Some were developed to serve such purposes as guarding, herding or some specialized form of hunting. The Greyhound's purpose was, and is, to run in packs after prey ranging in size from rabbits to deer. With few exceptions, Greyhounds will not guard or protect and, while in pursuit, they will not come if called. Most Greyhounds prefer not to swim, fetch or jump in the air for a Frisbee — it just isn't in their genes. What is in their genes is their size (large), their shape (aerodynamic) and their instinct to run in cooperation with other Greyhounds. Combine this with the chasing-reinforcement training that racing dogs receive in their formative years, and you have a large, streamlined, mild-mannered dog who can never be allowed off-lead except in fenced areas. Does this sound like the dog for you?

DO YOU HAVE ENOUGH SPACE?

As for the Greyhound's size, even though I tell people that Greyhounds are small large dogs (rather like the seeming contradiction of the name Little Big Horn), what I mean by that is that they are graceful, short-coated and often curl up in a tight ball when they sleep. Because of that they don't have as much of a physical presence as, say, a Newfoundland or a St. Bernard. They are, however, undeniably bigger than a Chihuahua or any of the many medium-size breeds. Do you have the space for those long legs, as well as the dog's crate, or will you and the Greyhound constantly be tripping over each other?

WHY GREYHOUNDS CANNOT RUN LOOSE

It is impossible to put too much emphasis on this point. There are some people who adopt who think that their dog is somehow different and can be trusted not to run away. Here are some facts, and a few sad anecdotes, that will illustrate why allowing a Greyhound to run free is a dangerous idea.

Greyhounds are among the fastest land mammals, with speeds reaching 41.72 mph. Horses, by comparison, have been known to reach 43.26 mph. If you think that you will simply run and catch your Greyhound if he bolts, consider this: a sprinting man can run only 27.89 mph. Therefore, catching a running Greyhound is only slightly less difficult than catching a running horse — which is to say, impossible.

Greyhounds have been bred for literally thousands of years for one thing: speed. If you think an obedience course is enough to wipe out eons of genetics and training, you are deluding yourself and risking your dog's life. In the case of retired racers, the situation is more acute because they have had the speed/chase mentality reinforced in them from the moment they were born. And, as we all know, what we learn as a child (or puppy) is what tends to stay with us for life.

Maddie, Rumi and Leggs, safe in a fenced yard.

Even before I began placing retired racers, I was drawn to them for their beauty and serenity. Every October I travel to New York City to attend the Feast of St. Francis at the Cathedral of St. John the Divine. On that day, all animals, from the huge elephant in the procession to the household pet, are welcome inside the church. The entire service is devoted to a celebration of animal life.

Every year I used to talk to a man who came all the way from Boston for the event with his two beautiful ex-racers. The dogs were so calm and loving that they would try to sit on his lap in the pew! Last year he came with only one dog. When I inquired about the other I heard the answer I feared: the dog was dead.

Despite warnings from the person he had adopted the dogs from, the man felt he knew his dogs well enough and had lived with them long enough (five years) that the advice to keep them on a lead no longer applied. Besides, he reasoned, the dogs had been obedience-trained. So, for several years he had been allowing them to run free in a large park in Boston well away from the park's boundaries. His version of Russian roulette worked quite well until that fateful day when a squirrel crossed the Greyhound's path. Perhaps the dog felt especially good that day. Perhaps some old chasing memory clicked inside his brain. For whatever reason, he took off and ignored the call of his owner. The boundary of the park meant nothing to the dog, and we can only hope that when he ran between two parked cars and into the path of a bus that his death was swift and painless.

Here's another tale, which, while obviously foolhardy, gives you another idea of what can happen:

A woman from Florida who had adopted a Greyhound almost a year earlier took her dog, unleashed, to a Fourth of July parade. Naturally there were crowds, the sounds of marching bands, and the occasional firecracker. It was a firecracker that so startled the otherwise calm dog that he took off. Several people tried to catch him, but his fear exceeded their speed. His dead body, obviously hit by a car, was found the next day 10 miles from the parade site.

So, if you adopt a Greyhound, are you willing to keep him leashed? He can run in your fenced yard, of course. And if you don't have a fenced yard, perhaps you have a friend or neighbor who would let you release your dog once or twice a week in their yard. Another alternative is a fully enclosed tennis court, football or baseball field. If none of the above is available, then make sure that when you adopt you seek out one of the less active Greyhounds up for adoption, one whose exercise needs can be satisfied by a good brisk walk once or twice a day. To choose otherwise is to set yourself up for frustration and failure.

GREYHOUNDS ARE COMPANIONS, NOT GUARD DOGS

If you are looking for a dog that will do double duty as both a pet and a protector, perhaps you should investigate other breeds. Greyhounds are very unaggressive dogs (remember, they were created to cooperate!), and the vast majority of them will not even bark when they see a stranger approaching the house. One of the remarks people often make after attending a gathering of Greyhounds is that the dogs are so quiet! They are watchdogs only in the sense that they will watch, but probably not act.

HOW TO CHOOSE YOUR IDEAL GREYHOUND

Now that I have done everything I can to make sure that you have a clear idea of what you are about to undertake, the next step is choosing *your* ideal Greyhound. Notice the emphasis on the word *your*. Keep in mind the expression "to each his own." The only ideal Greyhound is the one who will meet your particular expectations and requirements. With that said, let's make a list of those traits desirable to you.

PERSONALITY

What type of personality would you like your dog to have?

A dog's personality must be at the top of everyone's list because no matter how beautiful (or needy) a dog may be, it is his personality that determines whether or not he will be happy with you, and you with him. While all Greyhounds share some traits in common, there are individual differences. Do you want an extremely affectionate dog? Some people find it charming when a dog follows them from room to room, others consider it annoying. Do you want a very intelligent dog? If you do, make sure you channel the energy into something constructive because brains left untrained can think up things to do that might not be pleasing to your sense of order. Do you want a very quiet dog? Companionable and low-key to one person may add up to dull and boring to another.

ACTIVITY LEVEL

What sort of activity level do you desire in your dog? Very peppy? A potential jogging companion? A couch potato?

Be realistic. If you adopt a very athletic, active dog with the thought that it will somehow inspire you to exercise, think about what your own track record has been. Do you have a basement full of exercise equipment that was bought on a whim and rarely used since? Do you have a kitchen full of dust-covered diet drinks or an unused health club membership? A very active Greyhound is not going to be happy if his only exercise is following you from the refrigerator to the recliner. If you are currently exercising regularly, then do, by all means, consider a Greyhound as a jogging companion. If, however, you expect him to inspire you, try the local gym first and see how long you stick with it.

Also, even if you are very active when you get home from work, but are gone from the house eight to ten hours a day, it is unrealistic to expect a very energetic dog to go into a state of suspended animation while you aren't around and then suddenly become a ball of fire the minute you step inside the door. Look

Greyhound activity ranges from this . . .

. . . to this!

for a dog that is injury-free but only moderately active. That way he'll be calm enough to doze off while you're gone, but able to do some long hikes or short jogs with you.

AGE

Do you have a preference as to the age of the dog?

Racing Greyhounds, because they had a relatively regimented early life, tend to mature emotionally somewhat slower than other dogs. For this reason, a two-year-old is often very much a puppy. Is that appealing to you, or would you prefer a dog that has already worked out such stages as chewing and jumping around? Also, remember that the life span of a Greyhound is from 12 to 14 years. Try to imagine where you will be 10 years from now. Perhaps you would be better off choosing a somewhat older dog. My experience has shown me that older dogs — from, say, five to six years — are even more grateful for their retirement homes and still have many good years ahead!

OTHER PETS

Do you have other pets? Does your ex-racer need to get along with your cats?

Generally speaking, other dogs are not a problem, but a small number of ex-racers see cats, birds and very little dogs as moving prey. Make sure you tell the adoption agency or the person running the kennel that your new dog must get along with your other pets. There can be no guarantees, of course, when you are dealing with animals, but the person in charge should be able to direct you to a dog that he or she is fairly certain will fit in with the rest of your family.

And, by the way, don't think that you will somehow train a dog out of the habit of lunging for cats. When the instinct is deeply ingrained, the only homes for these few are ones without small pets. Some groups try electric shock collars to "deprogram" the dogs, but I find the method to be a cruel and extremely crude way to train. Don't try it! There are plenty of homes without small pets that are perfect for the dyed-in-the-wool chasers, so there's really no reason to force the issue!

Ajax and Phoebe, an Airedale, in interbreed rapport.

Another thing to remember is that just because a dog is not small-animal friendly, it has no bearing on how he will be as a pet. I have known cat-safe Greyhounds that were indifferent to people, and Greyhounds that had a high prey drive yet were devoted family pets. It depends on the dog.

King relaxing with friends Daniel,
Clawdia (foreground) and Alice (background).

CHILDREN

Do you have children who live with you or who visit often? If you do, and if they are very young, are you willing to supervise their interactions?

No dog is foolproof around kids, but some seem to enjoy the activity of children, while others would rather be left alone. As I said in the introduction, most Greyhounds are inherently kind, but you must not try their patience by allowing children to do whatever they want to them or any other pet. I am not only referring to children who are overtly aggressive with pets by doing such things as pulling their ears. I also mean children who are constantly falling over or stepping on the dog, or ones who will just never let the dog rest. Dogs can't tell whether something that is annoying them is intentional or accidental, and they really don't care. All they know is that it's a source of irritation. Even a dog who is a living saint can be pushed to snap, given the right stimulus. For this reason, if you have children age six or younger, I do not recommend adopting a Greyhound, or any breed of dog, unless you are 100 percent committed to protecting the dog from the children and the children from the dog. In practical terms, what this means is that they should not be left alone together unless you are supervising them. No exceptions.

My experience has been that young male Greyhounds have more tolerance for children than do the females. I believe the reason for this is that females tend to regard children as puppies. It is in their nature to discipline their own puppies when they get too boisterous, and some do the same with human children. This is usually evidenced by growling or barking when their patience has been pushed to the limit. Males, on the other hand, tend to see children as siblings. Males play more actively, so a rough-and-tumble session is what they expect.

The presence of children or grandchildren in the home is a fact that you must reveal to the person handling the adoption. And if you are picking out the dog in person, by all means bring your children along so you can judge the dog's reaction to them.

COMPANION OR PROTECTOR?

Are you looking just for a companion or for a companion and protector?

By nature Greyhounds are not aggressive animals, so, for guard duty, they are not ideal. There are some that will bark when a stranger approaches the house and that, coupled with their size, might be enough to deter someone with the idea of breaking in, but barkers are in the distinct minority. In big cities where there tend to be more guard dogs, I have noticed people watching me and my dog approach them on the street and actually crossing to the other side as we get close, and then crossing back again after we pass. This is amusing because my dogs look to me for protection! From adopting out these dogs I have had more than a few people tell me that they are afraid of black dogs (I personally find them to be the most beautiful). So, if you want a dog that commands respect, you might consider a black one, but please remember that they are, in fact, no more aggressive than dogs of any other color.

SIZE

Is size a consideration?

Think about the size of your house, your yard and even your car. The smallest female can weigh as little as the mid-40s. The largest male can reach the mid-90s. Both cases are rare. Generally the females range from 50 to 60 pounds and the males from 65 to 75 pounds. Obviously a Greyhound, even a relatively small one, is going to take up more room than, say, a Fox Terrier. The largest male we ever placed was Conor, whose racing weight was 105 pounds. The smallest female was Wee Wicked, whose weight was 40 pounds. Both dogs represent the extreme, not the average. Greyhounds are, however, graceful dogs that seem to know how to tuck themselves into small spaces. Most people who see a Greyhound for the first time consider them huge, but after a while they get used to their size and realize that Greyhounds are basically all legs!

Fiona demonstrates how Greyhounds can tuck into small spaces.

GENDER

Do you have a preference as to the gender of the dog?

Because there are already more Greyhounds than there are homes for them, responsible adoption agencies will either require you to spay or neuter your new dog, or they will have it done in advance. If altering the dog is up to you, bear in mind that it is less expensive to neuter a male than it is to spay a female. And, in case you were wondering, adult male Greyhounds are not more aloof than the females and are every bit as affectionate! The only difference between a neutered male and a spayed female is that, in most cases, the males are larger. Beyond that, it's just a matter of personal preference.

If you already have a dog (either a Greyhound or any other breed) and you are planning to add a Greyhound to your family, it is generally a safe bet to have a male and female together. In those cases, it is usually the female that becomes dominant. With two females together there is sometimes a bit of jockeying for position (the same can be true of two males), but it usually works out.

Don't believe what you've heard about male dogs not getting along. You can imagine that I pretty much have my choice of any dog, yet my present pack consists of four males and two females. The main thing to keep in mind is matching their temperaments. If they get along, then it doesn't matter what sex they are.

I am always astonished when people applying to adopt a Greyhound from me insist on a female because they are sure that males will urinate in the house. I am quick to point out that males are every bit as easy to housebreak as females. Furthermore, if a dog of either sex is soiling the house, it is the fault of the owner, not the dog. A housebroken dog may have an accident if he is under stress or brought into a new environment. But such a scenario could just as easily occur with a female as with a male. I'm sure my four "clean as wax" males would be mortally offended if they knew how their entire gender was being falsely accused!

Sophie (left), a female, and Ajax, a male.

Three males in harmony: Ajax (front), Jasper (back left) and King.

COLOR

Do you have a color preference?

As I said in the beginning, looks should be your last consideration because, once the dog is yours, trust me, it will suddenly become the most beautiful dog in the world. There is a wide array of Greyhound colors including black, white, fawn (tan), cream, red (rust), many shades of brindle (striped) and white with either red, fawn, black or brindle patches. The one color you will rarely see is grey (called blue). Whether it is fact or fiction, the feeling in the racing world is that the blue dogs are not good runners. For that reason they are seldom available for adoption after retirement because most never raced to begin with! Many in the racing world also feel that the blue dogs are prone to cancer and skin problems. Again, although I could find no facts to back up the prejudice against blue dogs, it is something to consider. After all, those within the industry have had lots of experience, and they should be in a position to know which dogs are the healthiest.

Again, keep in mind that you are adopting a dog to save his life. Would you really consider a dog less worthy of adoption, or less loveable, because of his color? If so, perhaps you should rethink your motivation for adoption.

CHOOSING AN ADOPTION AGENCY

Now that you have made a list of the traits you are looking for in a Greyhound, how do you decide which of the many groups that are out there can be trusted to help you make this important, life-time commitment to a dog?

My advice is, just as the adoption group should interview you, you should interview the group. Let's face it: All groups get their Greyhounds from the same sources, so none can claim truthfully that their dogs are somehow superior to others (and, even if they did use that ploy, who would be attracted by it?). What can be superior, however, is a group's experience, their care in making matches, their post-adoption support and their ability to do it all cheerfully and responsibly. Pretend you are hiring someone for a job (which, in a way, you are). For the sake of comparison, inter-view more than one group. For the sake of the group (which, most likely is staffed by volunteers), limit your formal application to one adoption agency. It is not fair to have a group spend time checking your references and finding you a dog, only to be told that you adopted one elsewhere.

It is important to ask a group representative the following questions:

- How long have they been in existence?
- How many dogs have they placed?
- What is the adoption fee?

- What, exactly, do you get for that fee?

- Do you choose a dog, or do they?

- If you choose, will someone tell you if they don't think you've picked the right dog for your particular situation?

- If they choose, are you free to decline or will you be obligated to take whoever is chosen for you?

- What happens if an adoption is not successful (for example, if a Greyhound turns out not to be cat-safe)?

- If they will take back their dog, will they do so in a reasonable amount of time (a day or two)?

- Will your adoption fee be refunded if the reason for a return was not your fault?

- What sort of post-adoption support does the group offer?

- Finally, how do you feel about the person you are speaking to? This is the intangible, but is very important. Just as no dog is right for every person, so, too, is no group right for every person. Remember, as well, that just because a group shares your views on racing (for, neutral or against), does not necessarily mean they are the right group for you to adopt from. You still need to know their adoption policies in advance. Since you may be dealing with this agency quite a bit (especially in the beginning), you must feel that they are listening to you and your needs and that they have your, and the dog's, best interest at heart.

THE ADOPTION PROCESS

There are innumerable ways to adopt a Greyhound. As I mentioned earlier, the two methods that are most common are visiting a kennel of retired racers or having an agency choose for you. Either method is fine as long as you stick to your list of requirements.

CHOOSING A DOG FROM A KENNEL

If you visit an adoption kennel, the staff there should be in a position to direct you to dogs who match what you are looking for. Because they take care of the dogs, they are likely to be familiar with each dog's temperament. Tell the person in charge exactly what traits you want. If he or she seems to disregard your request and attempts to push a wild-eyed youngster on you when you specifically said you wanted a companion for your retirement years, either ask to speak to someone else, or leave. Likewise, if you just came in to look and you feel pressured to adopt, leave. Finally, I would like to think that a person in charge of a kennel would sense if you were adopting on a whim and would have the integrity to suggest that, at the very least, you sleep on your decision. Beware: Those who make it too easy to adopt a dog may make it very hard to return one.

I suggest making several visits to a kennel before reaching your final decision. Granted, you will be seeing the dogs in an environment unlike your home, but you may pick up some

Will you be able to resist the pleading eyes of a Greyhound who needs a home?

important information this way. Perhaps your first visit should be adults only. On the second visit, you can bring any children who might be living with the dog. On the third visit, you might ask if you can bring your dog from home to see how the two interact in a quiet area. If either dog is aggressive with the other, or extremely frightened of the other, this might not be a good match. By the way, you must abide by the kennel's rules. A ban on bringing in other dogs, or a flock of children, does not mean the kennel is unprofessional. It may simply be a matter of insurance or may be too disruptive to their overall operation.

I might as well warn you right now that when it comes time to make a decision, it will be hard. Nothing is more appealing than the soulful look in a Greyhound's eyes staring at you from behind the wire mesh of a crate. My advice? Stand firm and remember what you are looking for. Again, several visits may be appropriate, as it will get you used to the kennel setting and it will give you a chance to think over the dogs who were "contenders" during your first visit.

MATCHMAKER, MATCHMAKER, MAKE ME A MATCH

If you are adopting sight unseen, you may actually be at an advantage because you won't be at the mercy of those pleading eyes. Matching a person with a dog is both an art and a science. How well an agency accomplishes that job is based on what you tell them you want, their perception of you, their experience, their knowledge of the dogs they are getting and, finally, their dedication. This is why it is essential that you feel comfortable with the group and that you trust their choice for you.

Faults in judgment can occur, of course, and sometimes a dog can behave one way in the kennel and quite differently in a home, but try to make sure the agency is really trying for a match and not just a placement. Make sure, too, that they are willing to take back, or exchange, a dog who just does not fit in with your lifestyle.

When It Just Isn't a Match

There are times when no amount of training, medication or patience will make an adoption work. In some cases, it is better for everyone concerned to either return, or exchange, a dog for one who is a better fit with your family. I do not recommend you take this step lightly — it should be done only after all other alternatives have been exhausted. Here are some of what I consider to be valid reasons.

If you find your Greyhound consistently avoids your children, you should consider exchanging her for one who is more enthusiastic about kids. Likewise, if your Greyhound consistently displays an aggressive posture to your children when they so much as enter a room, it might be wise to exchange the dog. Needless to say, if the dog has attacked without provocation, or simply cannot be trusted to play gently, an exchange is in order. If, however, your dog has growled or barked at your children in response to intentional aggression (hitting the dog) or accidental aggression (falling on the dog), you can choose to supervise more carefully and can use the occasion as a lesson for your children that dogs have feelings too!

If your Greyhound is truly not safe with your cats or small dogs, you are doing everyone a grave disservice by keeping a high prey-drive Greyhound. Your small animals should not have to be segregated for the rest of their lives, nor should the Greyhound be continually segregated (and frustrated).

If your Greyhound simply cannot adjust to living as an only dog, you need either to get another dog or return her. To medicate a dog into a stupor when there are other alternatives available is just not fair to the dog. In a similar vein, some dogs have a greater need for human companionship than do others. If your schedule requires long and frequent absences and you find that your Greyhound is in anguish about this, returning him would enable him to be placed in a situation that can better satisfy his needs.

Choose a dog with your head and your heart.

FIRST IMPRESSIONS: WHAT YOU MIGHT NOTICE AND WHAT TO LOOK FOR

Regardless of whether you choose your dog or he is chosen for you, it is helpful if you can get some idea of a dog's history, and, with any luck, his medical history. Bear in mind, however, that for some dogs, such information is nonexistent. Not all trainers are

34

good record-keepers. Many dogs, for example, receive their yearly inoculations but no records are kept. Some adopters mistakenly assume that trainers keep a "baby book" of each dog's first training session or first winning race. The fact is that many records are kept in the trainer's head. When time is short and staffing is inadequate, many kennels concentrate on the most immediate demands on their time — feeding, cleaning up and training. Record-keeping under these circumstances can become a luxury. Adoption groups always request medical histories, but they do not always receive them. If this turns out to be the case with the dog you have selected, you should at least receive the latest inoculation record. And, as with choosing any dog, look for clear eyes, a clean nose and no obvious signs of illness or injury.

Broken legs, broken toes and pulled ligaments are not uncommon injuries in the racing world. Some dogs recover fully from such ailments, while others may be left with a limp ranging from slight to pronounced. Some injuries can be corrected by surgery. If such a handicap is a minor flaw to you, then I encourage you to select one of these deserving Greyhounds, as most potential adopters, and, sadly, many adoption groups, will overlook dogs with any defects.

If you are choosing a female, try to find out if she was on hormones to prevent her heat cycle, and, if she was, for how long. If she wasn't, find out when she had her last heat. As with medical records, this sort of information is not always available. Unless you are told otherwise, assume that a female was on hormones and that, once off, she could go into heat at any time (although, in a minority of cases, females who have been on hormones never go into heat again). It is not at all uncommon, when we take in a shipment of dogs, for a female to go into heat in the truck on her way to us. When one female goes into heat, it is also common for the other females on board to follow suit. When that is the case, you must wait for about a month after the bleeding has subsided to have her spayed.

Of course you need to know if the dog has already been spayed or, in the case of males, neutered and, if so, when. It is estimated that it takes 30 days for the hormone level in a dog's body to adjust to being altered, so, especially in the case of males, allow for some of the more typical male behavior to subside gradually after neutering.

Other questions to ask are how recently the dog was retired as well as why he was retired. If he was retired because of an injury, find out what kind. This is especially important if you plan on participating in certain sports with the dog, such as artificial lure coursing. The dog may be in perfect health, but some injuries may preclude certain activities. If you are simply planning to nurture a house pet, don't let a minor racing injury bother you. Most will never affect a dog that simply takes walks with his owner or even one that races around the backyard. But, if you are planning vigorous exercise with your Greyhound, tell the adoption person in advance.

One other point concerning the racing career is how well the dog did on the track. Often a dog that did extremely well is treated differently (better) than the other dogs. This will sometimes affect the dog's behavior in retirement.

Take the case of Amber. While she was in the foster home awaiting adoption, she literally took over the house. She demanded to be the first one fed, she took everyone's toys away from them and she snatched the softest bed away from one of the long-time residents. When, on the rare occasion that she was reprimanded, she pouted for hours afterward. It was quite unusual for a new dog to be so bossy, but when we discovered that she had been a champion at the track as well as the trainer's favorite, suddenly it all made sense. She was spoiled, plain and simple!

It is hard to generalize about what you are likely to encounter with a new dog off the track. The first thing that comes to mind, however, is a bald bottom. Many of them have had the hair worn off the back and sides of their legs from rubbing against the walls of the crates they are housed in. This is nothing to worry about. Most dogs start growing hair back within a few weeks. Please do not jump to the conclusion that this is a sign of an underactive thyroid. If that were the case, there would be a uniform hair loss

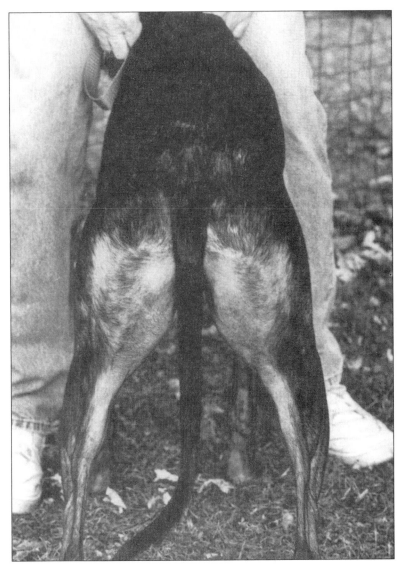

Typical baldness from crate rubbing at the track.

all over the body not to mention many other symptoms. Before beginning a potentially dangerous, lifetime course of supplements, read the thyroid material in Chapter Five.

Another thing that is sometimes seen is skin irritation on the chest. This is caused by blocked pores (blackheads) — the result of dogs lying in the sand of the turnout pen. The problem can be treated easily by applying warm compresses to the area then gently squeezing the clogged pores or by applying an ointment from your vet. You can, of course, leave it alone, as it causes no pain to the dog. Incredibly, some people have suggested cutting out the affected flesh from the chest of dogs who have this condition. By no means should you subject your dog to the hazards of anesthesia, and post-surgical pain, simply for the sake of appearances. This is not only bad medicine, but also inhumane.

Occasionally we will see a dog fresh off of the track with one or both elbows swollen. The swelling resembles a golf ball under the skin. The cause of this condition is inadequate bedding, and the best treatment we have found is to just leave it alone. In three to four weeks time the swelling subsides and the dog once again has a normal appearance. We have known of veterinarians who have attempted to aspirate the fluid, and in every case, the condition has worsened. Yes, the swelling is unsightly. No, it is not painful, so if you just have patience and give the dog plenty of bedding, the swelling should go away on its own.

People sometimes erroneously assume that a dog with scars is a fighter. This is probably not the case. After all, racing Greyhounds are muzzled almost all the time. Scars can be the result of a pile-up on the track or even the result of a loose wire on a fence or on the door of their crate. Even if the scars were the result of a fight, which is most unlikely, remember that it is generally the victim that winds up with scars, not the aggressor.

As for personality testing, the best recommendation I can give is to opt for a dog with a moderate personality. Choose neither the most active nor the most subdued. Sometimes the overly active dog can be too much to handle for the average owner. Likewise, the overly subdued, submissive type can become panic-stricken when frightened (and it often doesn't take much to get a dog in that state). A simple, mild-mannered, uncomplicated dog generally makes the best pet.

A Greyhound will reward you with never-ending affection . . .

. . . and will be your best friend.

FOLLOW YOUR HEAD AND YOUR HEART

Now that you have the ideal Greyhound (for you) in mind, here's a little advice that may seem contradictory to all I've said so far: be flexible. Try to get the most important qualities you are looking for, but if one dog catches your eye and you make a connection, give the dog a chance. Perhaps the dog is a little smaller than you wanted, and maybe he doesn't seem quite as smart, but there is a lot to be said for the chemistry that sometimes occurs between a person and a dog. Go with your head and heart.

Chapter Three

The Racing Life

*I*n order to understand fully why your ex-racer acts the way he does, it is helpful to know where he came from and how he is used to living life. Many of his current habits are the direct result of years of training. Knowing why he does something can assist you in changing any of his behaviors that you find undesirable or in reinforcing good behavior.

THE BUSINESS ARRANGEMENTS

Racing kennels are often, but not always, located in a compound on the grounds of the Greyhound racetrack. Each kennel is owned by a different person who, in most cases, hires a trainer. The kennel owners are responsible for all the bills (food, veterinary fees and so on) that a dog incurs and for paying wages to the trainer and kennel helpers. The trainer is responsible for training a dog and for deciding which races a dog will enter and when. The owners pay nothing toward a dog's maintenance at the track, but when a dog earns money, a standard arrangement is that the kennel owner gets 65 percent of the winnings (5 percent of which is paid to the trainer), while the owner gets 35 percent. In a typical kennel, dogs from many different owners are housed and trained together.

Many owners own lots of different dogs and can have them under contract to kennels all over the country. Likewise, many owners never even meet their dogs. They can buy and sell their racers over the phone.

Golly Wally communicates with his trainer, Louis Palazzo.

To a great extent, owners of a racing dog must rely on trust in the kennel owner and trainer. Often they take the trainer's word for it when they are advised to buy or sell a dog. They also must trust the kennel owner to provide proper veterinary care and nutrition for the dog. In the majority of cases, the trainers treat the dogs well in the hopes that the dogs will, in turn, perform well on the track.

THE DAILY ROUTINE

Racing kennels consist of double-deck banks of crates along the inside walls of the building with an aisle down the middle. Standard crate size is 2½ feet wide, 3 feet high and 3½ feet deep. The preferred bedding is shredded newspaper, since it provides both insulation and a deep cushion. Both are very important, as Greyhounds, which have very little hair and virtually no fat to act as padding, are easily chilled and prone to pressure sores when exposed to hard surfaces.

The day begins early at the track, and the same routine is repeated without variation. Generally the dogs are turned out for the first time at 6 or 6:30 in the morning. Three more turnouts follow in a day: 10 A.M., 4 P.M. and 9 P.M. The turnout pen is divided into two sides, one for the males and one for the females. The dogs are always turned out with their muzzles on to prevent any confrontations. As will be described in detail in Chapter Seven, "Training," these are not their racing muzzles but, rather, a smaller, lighter type used solely for turnout and traveling.

A typical arrangement of crates: turnout muzzles,
made of lightweight wire or plastic, hang on doors.

Jill in her crate at the adoption kennel.

While the dogs are relieving themselves and stretching their legs, the trainers and their helpers are busy cleaning any of the crates that have been soiled during the night. Most Greyhounds do not soil their crates, but accidents do happen.

THE HANDLING OF THE DOGS

When the dogs are brought in, perhaps 30 to 40 minutes later, each one is checked before being put back into the crate. The average kennel houses about 40 dogs (although there can be as many as 75 to 100), and the trainer must know each one. The length and condition of their toenails and pads are checked, their

44

eyes and ears are examined and, by lifting the dog into the crate and giving it the once-over, the trainer can tell if a dog is getting enough or too much to eat. Because of these frequent examinations, Greyhounds are used to being handled. Even as pups on the farm they are handled daily for such things as weighing, deworming or being led to the turnout pen.

THEIR MUSICAL BACKGROUND

One constant I have observed in every racing kennel is the sound of music — nonstop, 24 hours a day. I personally found it a bit maddening (especially some of the radio stations chosen), but I suppose you can get used to anything after a while. It was explained to me that the music serves two purposes. First, it calms the dogs and provides yet another constant in their life. Second, it helps drown out noises from the outside. If, for example, a truck pulled up during the night, all of the dogs would assume they were about to be turned out and would get up and

Chris Makepeace turning out the female Greyhounds.
The males are on the other side of the fence.

bark. Pretty soon the entire racing compound would be awake and barking. Racing dogs need their rest, so, as strange as it may seem, the music is always on.

FEEDING

Food is extremely important in a racing kennel, both in quantity and quality. Racing Greyhounds have what is known as a set weight, which is basically the weight at which they look good and run well. Maintaining that weight is an art and a science, and there are as many different opinions on how to achieve it as there are racing kennels.

Dogs are not fed the day they are raced. A dog is not permitted to run on a full stomach because it can cause gastric torsion. Instead, dogs are given a few biscuits to tide them over until after the race.

TRAINING

By the time a dog has reached racing age, at approximately 17 months, he has already had a good deal of training. Some of it came naturally, some was man-made.

Most racing Greyhounds are born on farms in the Midwest and in Florida. Bitches that have been bred are kept in special brooding kennels away from the other dogs. A few hours before she gives birth, the bitch makes an elaborate nest in her brooding box. Greyhounds are known for their keen maternal instincts, and rarely will a bitch reject her litter. Some bitches are still producing litters at 10 to 12 years of age, although humane treatment would suggest an earlier retirement from motherhood. At birth, Greyhound puppies look like any other little dogs, and it is not until they are about three months of age that the distinctive long legs and long muzzle develop.

The pups are weaned by their mothers when they are eight to nine weeks old. By that age, their teeth and claws are surprisingly sharp. Although the pups are separated from their mothers, they are not separated from each other. In fact, a litter of pups, which

Trainer John Ard prepares enormous quantities of food.

can range in number from one to sixteen, but averages six to eight, usually remains together until they are eight to ten months old. The reason for this, in part, is because the pups help to train

At nine weeks of age, a Greyhound pup doesn't look much like a Greyhound.

each other. At weaning age their ears are tattooed, which identifies them for the racing business.

At commercial breeding farms, young pups are turned out in fenced runs that are 250 to 300 feet long. As young as two months, pups begin racing with each other up and down the length of the runs. In good weather they are out for 20 to 30 minutes at a time, and if you watch them closely, you can see them already competing with each other.

At six months of age their training begins in earnest. Most trainers start out by tying a plastic jug to a rope, pulling it along the ground and having the pups chase it. Later on, a jug or an animal pelt is pulled along by a slow-moving tractor. Still later the dogs run after an artificial lure suspended on a whirligig, and finally, they run in simulated racetrack conditions. Although it is illegal in most states to train the Greyhounds on a live lure, such as a rabbit, the practice still persists in some areas. Some old-time dog trainers swear that until a dog has tasted blood he's no good at the track. Of course, such cruel myths have no basis in fact, to which racing records will attest.

A Greyhound first gets a collar around his neck at four months of age. From the age of about eight months, Greyhounds learn to walk on a lead. The reasons for this early training are obvious: Their entire lives are spent being led from one place to another. With so many dogs to handle, a trainer cannot waste time with a dog that pulls or stops frequently. This training holds them in good stead when they become companions, too.

THEIR FIRST RACE

The first professional race a Greyhound competes in is called his maiden race. Maidens are reserved for dogs, males or females, that have never won a race before. Typically races have eight dogs, but occasionally there are nine. The average age at which a Greyhound runs his maiden race is 18 months.

Speed is not the only factor that determines which dog will win. A dog must possess endurance and agility, too. If a dog bursts from the starting box with all of his might and holds no energy in reserve, he may well finish last. A dog must also concentrate on the lure and, simultaneously, keep his eyes on the other dogs so he doesn't accidentally bump into them. A pileup on the track could result in serious injuries and, of course, slows everyone down. Finally, a dog must not be guilty of interference, which means that he must not purposely bump other dogs or start fights with them.

A young Greyhound is given six chances to come in first, second, third or fourth in a maiden race. If he does not accomplish this, he is either "retired" and put up for adoption or is euthanized. I wonder how many of the betting public know that a young dog's very life can depend on whether he wins, places or shows in a race.

ASCENDING THE RANKS

Assuming that all goes well and that a dog finally wins a maiden race, he is then promoted to Grade J, which is for dogs that have just won the maiden. Other grades, from A to D, depend on how a dog places after each race he runs. Generally speaking, a dog gradually ascends the grades, then, as he ages and slows down, descends. The difference in speed, by the way, between a Grade-A dog and a Grade-D dog can be as little as ¾ of a second.

King (Low Key Two), on the left, and his littermate
Tim (Counterpoint Two), shown here with turnout muzzles,
both ran and won in Grade A at major tracks. (Photo: Charlotte Mosner)

KEEPING RACING HONEST

Every dog that wins a race has his urine analyzed for the presence of illegal drugs. Forbidden substances include butazolidin (an anti-inflammatory), stimulants, depressants, steroids and even aspirin. Ninety-seven drugs can be detected by the tests, the object of which is to keep racing honest. In addition to the winner, one other dog is picked at random after each race to be tested.

Racing bitches are every bit as fast as the dogs. To prevent them from going into heat (which would not only slow them down but would cause the dogs to riot back at the kennel), they are given testosterone. When their racing careers are over and they are taken off the hormone, many females go into heat immediately while others never go into heat again (see Chapter Two, "Choosing the Right Dog for You").

Usually there are 13 to 15 races in a day, and an individual dog is run only once every three to four days. By the time a dog reaches the finish line he has burned up all the available carbo-hydrates in his body. R and R is greatly needed.

At the finish line the dogs, wearing no collars — only racing muzzles and numbered blankets — are caught by the person who led them onto the track and are handed over to someone from the dog's kennel. The dog is walked for a few minutes to cool down and is taken back to the kennel to rest and drink water. An hour or so after the race the dog is fed. In most kennels, a dog that has won is given a special treat. The ones that don't win are, lit-erally, in the dog house.

RACING INJURIES

There are several hazards that a racing dog faces on the track. Some injuries can lead to retirement, while others can lead to death. When you consider the tremendous speeds that these dogs can reach, it is a wonder that broken legs are not more common. With luck, and proper veterinary care, a leg can be set and a dog can eventually resume racing. For others, though, a break can be so severe that they can never race again. Some injuries are caused by dogs bumping into each other and others are caused by unsafe track conditions. Perhaps the worst possible accident for dogs is electrocution from falling into the cradle that holds the electric lure. Thankfully, this is a relatively rare occurrence.

Other common injuries are torn ligaments, broken bones, pulled tendons, dislocated toes and various cuts, scrapes and bruises. One injury peculiar to Greyhound racing is known as a spike. Spikes occur by accident during the course of a race when the toenail of one dog punctures the back of the leg or foot of another dog. If untreated the puncture can become infected, but, when treated properly, it is a minor, albeit painful, mishap.

A veterinarian is present at each race and is responsible for all the dogs that are running. His duties can range from setting a broken leg, to putting a dog to sleep, to treatment for heat exhaustion.

As mentioned before, when you adopt an ex-racer, try to find out exactly why he was retired. If he just wasn't fast enough, that's one thing. But if he was retired due to an injury, it may prevent him from participating in certain activities. This is especially important if you want to adopt a dog to accompany you while jogging or to take lure coursing.

Racing Greyhounds can reach speeds over 40 m.p.h.
(Photo: National Greyhound Association)

*Ajax takes a walk down Memory Lane as he visits his old
boarding school — the Seabrook, New Hampshire, Race Track.
Although he was glad to see Chris Makepeace again,
he was equally glad to go home!*

A DAY IN A RACING DOG'S LIFE

From this chapter, you now know certain things about how racing dogs live and are trained. To sum up, the following generalizations can be made:

- Racing dogs are used to rising early.

- Racing dogs are used to a strict routine.

- Racing dogs are used to being handled.

- Racing dogs are used to music.

- Racing dogs are used to walking obediently on a lead.

- Racing dogs are used to being around other racing dogs.

- Racing dogs are used to four turnouts daily.

- Racing dogs are used to being around people.

Remember, the more you know about your dog's past, the better equipped you will be to give him the best future possible.

Chapter Four

In a Home

When bringing a retired racer into your home for the first time, the one thing to keep in mind is that everything is completely new to him. I don't just mean that the surroundings are unfamiliar, I mean that being in a house is a new experience. Also new is riding in a car (as opposed to a kennel truck), being around more people than dogs, climbing stairs, looking out windows, adapting to your routine and a myriad of other things that we regard as commonplace.

Racing Greyhounds lead a very insular life. From the time they are born until the day you bring them home, the only life they know is that of the kennel. They might as well be from another planet as far as their knowledge of the "real" world goes. Take heart, though. Greyhounds are not only very intelligent animals, they are also very intuitive. As such, their adjustment period is probably shorter than it would be for other breeds.

SEPARATION ANXIETY

As I said earlier, Greyhounds are dogs that have been bred to get along with other animals. Consequently, they tend to blend in with other pets that you might have. However, if you have no other pets, particularly no other dogs, being alone may be a little scary for your Greyhound. You see, never before have they been without other dogs, and sometimes they are initially over-whelmed by the fact that there is no other canine to reassure them.

In most cases, the Greyhound will transfer his desire for companionship to you. In practical terms, what this means is that you can expect the dog to follow you from room to room until he becomes accustomed to his new home and routine. My dog, King, was so intent on keeping me within sight that for the first few months he would even follow me into the bathroom! At the time he was the only dog I had. By the time I adopted my second Greyhound, Ajax, I not only still had King, but I had also adopted a stray Afghan Hound named Jasper.

TWO'S COMPANY

I suspect that the reason Ajax never clung to me as much as King did is that he came into a multi-dog family. Don't get me wrong — Ajax is very affectionate and would always choose to be with me rather than stay home, but he never exhibited a need for my company, merely the desire. If you are having excessive difficulty acclimating your new Greyhound to being left alone, do consider getting another dog, preferably another Greyhound. It may seem inconceivable to you, if you are having trouble with one, that getting another will actually be easier, but, believe me, it often works wonders!

Some cases of so-called separation anxiety are really just a part of your new pet getting settled in to your routine. One of the best things you can do during the first week or so that you have your dog is to take time off from work. That way you can help him adjust to life at your house. Keep in mind that you will get out of the relationship only as much as you put into it. Many people comment on how calm and well-acclimated my dogs are, but I am quick to point out that they didn't necessarily come that way. It takes time, patience and training.

If you are able to take some time off, make sure you spend part of that time away from the dog. While that may sound like a contradiction, it's very important to your dog's acclimatization. I have dubbed the following behavior the Schoolteacher Syndrome, because every spring I am approached by teachers who want to adopt a Greyhound after the school term is over so that they can spend the entire summer with the dog. I used to think this was a good idea too until I realized that what they were actually doing was putting off the inevitable. When the school term rolled around again, that's when the dogs would have the separation problems and that's when I would get the calls that I would normally expect to get from someone who had a dog for a few days rather than a few months. There is no point in getting the dog used to your being around full-time when, in fact, after a

Most Greyhounds are comforted by the presence of other dogs.

week or after a summer you're going to be back at work. Spend part of each day away so the dog can get used to being alone and to knowing that when you go out, you also come back.

While it is tempting to make a big fuss over your dog when you come home, try to resist. Stay calm and nonchalant. If you gush over the dog and tell him everything is okay, you are reinforcing the idea that everything was not okay while you were gone. The truth is, you need to have a life and you need to be able to leave your house. Your dog needs a life too, so try not to make a big deal of either coming or going.

To make life easier for him while you are gone, try duplicating the "mood music" that the racing kennels use. Some people have found that talk radio is effective, while others claim television works best.

Toys, especially of the stuffed variety, may be comforting to him, as may be an item of your clothing with your scent on it. To keep him busy, get a sterilized, hollowed-out marrow bone and stuff the center with either peanut butter or soft cheese. The idea is that the dog will spend the day trying to get the treat out from the center. You can restuff it every day if he happens to have cleaned it out, but that is unlikely. The filling should be buried deep enough to have a tantalizing scent but be just out of reach

They say a tired dog is a good dog, so before you leave for an extended period try to give your dog a good run or a brisk walk. If that isn't always possible, then play with him at home by tossing toys around the living room or getting him to follow you up and down the steps. It's a great workout for you, too!

If possible, get a friend, relative, neighbor or dog-walking service to take your dog out midday. While a dog can technically "hold it" for many hours, the emotional contact midday is useful and is especially helpful during the critical first few weeks. Whoever you get for that job, make sure he or she understands about never letting the Greyhound off-lead. This includes professional dog walkers as well. They must understand that the ex-racer is not like a Golden Retriever or German Shepherd.

Have you considered the possibility that you may be able to bring your dog to work? In some settings that would be impossible, of course, but in others, who knows? Perhaps there are no dogs where you work because no one ever thought to ask. Also, is there someone in your neighborhood who doesn't work or who works at home? Perhaps that person would enjoy dog-sitting for you while you're gone. A Greyhound could be a great companion for a retired person who might not want the commitment of a dog full-time but would love to spend the day with one. Get creative.

Only rarely does a Greyhound have a clinical case of separation anxiety. In this circumstance, the dog cannot be crated or he will hurt himself, but if he is left out, he will destroy the house. The answer is either to find a way that the dog will never be alone (a virtual impossibility) or to take the dog to a veterinary behaviorist who will prescribe a combination of specific desensitization training methods and a low dose of either an anti-anxiety drug or an anti-depressant. I cannot stress enough that this is the method of last resort. Too many people, and, sadly, too many veterinarians, are quick to give a dog a pill if he is not instantly acclimating perfectly. Like people, some dogs just take a little longer than others to adjust to new situations, and some are naturally less outgoing than others. It does not mean something is wrong with them. Remember: Time, patience and training cure most problems. Low doses of drugs can work wonders, but should only be considered after all else has failed. Even then, they should be prescribed only in conjunction with behavioral training and a complete physical examination.

In an ideal world, we could all stay home with our dogs and never have to leave them. In reality, though, most of us work away from home. What does this mean to a dog that is unsure of himself? That all depends on how you approach your absences.

HOW NOT TO BEGIN

Let me give you the worst-case scenario first.

A couple adopts a Greyhound, fresh off the track, on a week-day afternoon. They spend the evening with the dog and half the neighborhood who always wanted to see what a Greyhound looks like up close. The dog is given pizza by a child, whose parents think it's funny. The couple, in all the commotion, forgets to take the dog out, so he lifts his leg against the wall. The dog is hit hard with a newspaper. Because the dog seems so subdued the next morning, the couple decides it's okay to allow him the run of the house when they go to work.

When they get home they find that not only was the dog not housebroken, but that he has eaten their bedspread and clawed the doors to shreds. He has drunk water from the toilet, which contained a cleaning solution that caused him to vomit on the sofa. He has also knocked the dishes from the drain board in the kitchen onto the floor (cutting himself in the process) and has left a trail of blood all over the house. At this point the dog is in a weakened condition and requires immediate veterinary care.

HOW TO AVOID PROBLEMS

Where did the couple go wrong?

The entire problem could have been avoided by the use of a dog crate.

In adopting out retired racers, I cannot stress strongly enough to people how the use of a crate will make their lives easier as well as ease the transition for their new dog. I don't know how many times I've been asked, "But isn't it cruel to keep a dog confined?" My answer is the same every time: "Isn't it more cruel to subject a dog to the many hidden hazards around an unfamiliar house? Isn't it more cruel to return the dog after a few days because you've found him unmanageable?" To paraphrase Robert Frost, "Good crates make good dogs."

HOW TO MAKE A GOOD START

Now here's how the above scenario should have gone.

A couple adopts a Greyhound, fresh off the track, on a weekday afternoon. They spend a quiet evening with the dog, allowing him to get used to them and his new surroundings gradually. Although all of their friends and neighbors are eager to stop by and meet the new addition to the family, the couple decides that the dog has enough to contend with just checking out his new home.

The dog is given a medium-size dinner and plenty of water, since dogs that have been recently transported are often dehydrated. The dog is taken out often, including within 20 minutes of eating and right before bed. Each time he defecates or urinates outside he is praised. If he does have an accident in the house he is told "No" firmly but without anger or shouting. He is never beaten for an accident.

Knowing that the dog is a little scared by all of the changes, the couple sets up a crate in their bedroom. The dog cries and whimpers initially, but after a half hour or so he quiets down and they all go to sleep.

The couple has arranged to take the next few days off from work — first the wife for two or three days, then the husband. That way the dog can get to know both of them equally and they can show him the ropes. Whenever they have to go out during the day without him, they put him in the crate, which is brought into the kitchen or living room during the day. Fresh water is always available in the crate. As time goes on and they are sure the dog is housebroken and will not destroy the house if left alone, the dog is weaned from the crate gradually.

That is an ideal scenario. Sometimes, however, the ideal is impossible. What if, for example, the couple was unable to take time off from work? In that case, perhaps someone can look in on the dog during a lunch break. Or what if someone in the family was sick when the dog arrived? Maybe a friend or neighbor can help out. If that isn't possible, you can advertise for (or ask your vet to recommend) a dog walker. Retired people often welcome the extra money and are glad for something to do. Also, music or a talk show left playing on the radio is often soothing to the new dog. Just do the best you can, introduce things gradually to your dog and, above all, have patience.

Again, in the case of my Ajax, I used the following method of allowing him free rein in the house while he was getting acclimated. The first four nights he slept in the crate. By the way, on the first night, as soon as I opened the door to the crate he practically ran in. The second night he walked in. The third night he walked in very slowly, and on the fourth night he needed a small push. By the fifth night I had observed him enough to know that he could be trusted to neither chase the cats nor fight with the other dogs. I told him he could sleep uncrated on a trial basis. He was perfect and has not spent a night in a crate since.

The first night will undoubtedly be the hardest. Many dogs cry with anxiety. Don't worry; eventually they stop. Having the crate in your bedroom helps. Bear in mind that it is only natural that a dog will express to you that he is feeling lonely or scared. Be kind, have compassion and put yourself in his position. Wouldn't you be upset if the situation were reversed and suddenly you were forced to live in a kennel surrounded by dogs and no people?

If you have trouble getting your Greyhound to go in the crate, you're not alone. I must have had hundreds of calls from people who have told me they were having the same trouble. I find it somewhat amusing to hear how quickly the dogs can size up someone with a weak will. Ex-racers have spent their entire lives in a crate, and while I can understand that they are eager to get a taste of freedom, they are fully capable of going in if they know you mean it. I am not suggesting that we duplicate their regimented existence at the track, but you need to remember that the crate is not a punishment. It is a useful training tool and a safe haven for your dog.

The real issue here is a matter of will: they do not want to go in the crate, and you want them to. So, who is in charge, you or the dog? It is unwise to let them make the decision on the crate issue for two reasons. First, it teaches them that they are in charge, not you. That is not the message you want to give. Second, you are crating them as much for their own good as for the sake of your house. An unhousebroken, nervous Greyhound could get hurt in your house if left alone too soon. The crate can protect him.

The following method of getting your dog in the crate is pretty foolproof. Lead him to the crate. Tell him to "kennel up" (a common phrase at the track). If he won't, snap your fingers and repeat the phrase using a firm voice. Do not shout, mind you, but do use a voice that means business. If he still won't, try a little shove. If he won't still, toss in a piece of something delectable

Maddie enjoys getting away from it all in her crate.

such as a small piece of ham or liverwurst. If he won't after that, I suspect you have not mastered the tone of authority. Try again, and imagine you are a busy trainer at a track. Believe me, the dogs go in their crates at the track and they will go in for you too!

63

CRATES

There are two basic types of crates: hard-molded plastic (the kind used for transporting dogs by air) and wire (often collapsible). Either type is acceptable but I much prefer the plastic type, for the following reasons. Plastic crates are less expensive, sometimes half the price of a wire crate. A plastic crate in a size suitable for a Greyhound can be bought for well under a hundred dollars from discount pet supply stores or catalogs. They are also more denlike, which is the atmosphere a crate is duplicating. But the biggest advantage is that they make escapes very rare. Whenever people call to tell me that their dog has broken out of a crate, I can practically put money on it that they use a wire crate. Plastic crates were designed for airline travel, and you can be sure that airlines do not want dogs running loose in the belly of the plane!

I have heard of two complaints about plastic crates that deserve discussion. Some say that plastic crates do not offer adequate ventilation. This is untrue, as they have a full wire door as well as ventilation slats on both sides. If a dog was left in the direct sun in a plastic crate, it would probably get uncomfortable.

Sophie in a wire crate that is too small.

That would be true of a wire crate too, but with the added disadvantage of no shade. (There are, by the way, battery-operated clip-on fans with rubber blades. These fans can be attached to the door of a crate and offer relief in extreme heat.) The other complaint about plastic crates is that they are big, bulky and, let's face it, not too attractive. Yes, although they are designed with top and bottom halves that are detachable (which makes storage easy), they are guilty of, shall we say, not adding to home decor. Just keep in mind how useful they are and you will soon view your big, ugly crate as your dog's (and your) best friend.

To give wire crates their due, they do have two advantages over plastic ones. Wire crates provide better visibility. This can sometimes be a comfort to an anxious dog. The other advantage is that they are collapsible, which can come in handy when you are traveling with your pet.

Most Greyhounds need a crate of the following dimensions: 27 inches wide by 40 inches deep by 30 inches high. This is often known as a 500-size crate. Some of the very large males may need the next larger size (a 700) with the following dimensions: 32 inches wide by 48 inches deep by 35 inches high. If you get one much bigger than is actually needed, you will increase the chances of the dog soiling his crate because he will have enough room to move away from the mess.

If, for some reason, you choose not to use a crate — and believe me when I tell you that this is not a good idea — then at least refrain from confining the dog to the bathroom and instead try the kitchen with a gated doorway and newspaper on the floor. Bathrooms tend to be too small and can cause a dog to feel claustrophobic and panicky, while basements are generally dark and give the dog the feeling of being shut off from the rest of the house. Many Greyhounds who were wrongly confined to a bathroom or basement have reacted with panic and have tried to gnaw their way out, damaging the woodwork and their mouths in the process. Never put your ex-racer in a garage! Remember, the idea is to acclimate your dog to become a part of the family. Garages are for cars, not for your companions.

WEANING FROM THE CRATE

All of the above must be combined with the rarest of commodities — common sense. If, when you feel the dog is trustworthy, you decide to leave him alone uncrated, you must make sure that the house is relatively dog-proof. Don't leave anything of value or anything that could potentially harm your dog within his reach. Scan each room in your house before you leave. If there is an irreplaceable photo of Great-Aunt Bertha on the coffee table, move it. Is that a can of caustic drain opener beneath the sink? Move it. Use your imagination as to what might interest your dog. You can be sure he will!

The weaning from the crate is a gradual process. Don't expect to leave your dog alone for eight hours on the first try. My experience with Ajax illustrates one way of approaching this. Since I work at home, it was a relatively easy process. He would be uncrated during the day except when I had to go out. After four or five days I began leaving him uncrated for very short periods, such as the 10 minutes it would take me to get a quart of milk at the corner store. The next day I would try him uncrated for 20 minutes while I ran a few errands. Within about 10 days I felt comfortable enough to leave him uncrated for several hours. So far, seven years later, he has never betrayed my trust.

OTHER CHALLENGES

Four things that may be obstacles to your new Greyhound are smooth or highly waxed floors (such as in the kitchen), windows, swimming pools and stairs. If you approach each obstacle with patience and understanding, it won't be an obstacle for long.

SMOOTH FLOORS

Most Greyhounds never walk on really smooth floors during their racing days. The surfaces in and around the kennel and track are mostly dirt, clay or sand. Some Greyhounds walk on smooth floors without a hitch. For others, however, it appears to be a terrifying ordeal.

My own kitchen floor is linoleum, although not terribly smooth and certainly not very shiny. Neither of my Greyhounds has any trouble with it. However, when I take Ajax with me to give speeches about Greyhound adoption to service organizations and clubs, the meetings are often held in municipal buildings with very smooth, highly polished floors. The first time we went out in tandem, I'm afraid he didn't come off as a very good "AmbassaDog." As we entered the hall it was as if Ajax was walking on ice. All four legs splayed out, and he had a lot of difficulty just standing upright, much less walking. With much coaxing, and with the use of a blanket on the floor, I was able to inch him across the room to the podium. Now he has the hang of it and could probably race around the room if given half a chance.

If your dog has trouble on smooth floors at home, get pieces of scrap carpeting that he can walk on. Scatter the patches on the floor so that there are small carpet-free areas that he must use. Gradually, over the course of the next few days, remove the pieces of carpet one by one, and you probably won't need them again. There is also a resin-based product on the market that you can spray on your dog's pads to help him get a better grip. I doubt it will ever become necessary to use, but if your dog is having an especially hard time, this product is available at pet supply stores and is made just for dogs' paws, so it is safe.

This may be a good time to check the length of your dog's toenails. Usually they are kept fairly short for racing, but it's possible that they have grown too long. It is very difficult for a dog to walk properly if his toenails are untrimmed. It throws the weight of the foot toward the heel and allows him less maneuverability. Unless you are an expert, I recommend taking him to your local grooming parlor for a trimming. An appointment is often unnecessary, it only costs a few dollars and your dog will feel better and walk better. Once you learn how to do it, a biweekly trimming will keep them in fine shape. You can also ask your veterinarian to trim your dog's nails during an office visit. Most will do it gratis. Cutting extremely long nails can require general anesthesia since it can be a painful procedure. Please, don't ever let them get that long.

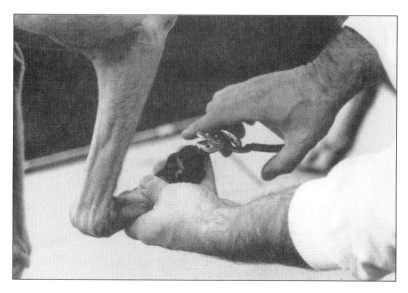

The correct way to trim toenails.

WINDOWS

At the racetrack, and in a kennel environment, racing Greyhounds have limited opportunity to actually look out a window. I'm not suggesting that they are kept in the dark, but they are generally either outside exercising or in the kennel building. Once inside, they mostly have a view from their crate onto an aisle facing other dogs. In the kennel trucks in which they are transported there are no windows, only louvers that can be opened for ventilation.

Because of this, windows are a new experience for your dog, and many are delighted with their expanded view of the world. It's hard to imagine how windows could pose a threat, but they can. Here are two examples of the many I've heard.

Before I adopted King he had been in several other adoptive homes. In the first home he had a near-fatal accident involving a window. He had only lived there two days when he was running around the house playing with the other dogs. In his excitement, King ran right through a sliding glass door because he didn't recognize it as something solid. He managed to sever an artery in his leg, and his owners got him to the vet just in time to save his life. He bears the scar to this day.

In another incident, a retired racer in North Carolina by the name of Logan leapt through a bedroom window in pursuit of a squirrel that was outside. She, too, was unaware of the fact that windows are solid. Fortunately she was unharmed, and I think her owner was more shaken by it than she was.

The point here is that it's a good idea to introduce your dog to any windows that he has even a remote chance of leaping through. The simplest way to teach him is simply to lead him over to the window and knock on it. You may also want to put his nose or paw against it so he can actually feel that it is solid. Some people put stickers or opaque tape on their windows, but I have found that the knocking/touching method works quite well. By the way, don't forget car windows!

DOG PROOFING YOUR STOVE AND WINDOW SHADE CORDS

As hard as it may be to believe, we placed one curious Greyhound who accidentally managed to turn on a gas range. How? He jumped up to see what was on the range and leaned on the knob. When he jumped down, his paw twisted the knob to the "on" position. Fortunately, his adopter was home and witnessed the scene. To make sure it never happened again, she bought a range-top guard designed to prevent small children from either turning on the range or from reaching up and burning themselves.

Another potential hazard is the cords that come with mini blinds or window shades. Unless they are tied off in the manner recommended by the manufacturer, they are as likely to choke a dog as they are to choke a child.

SWIMMING POOLS

In-ground swimming pools are very common in some parts of the country. Naturally, Greyhounds are unfamiliar with them and, as with windows, they need a guided tour in order to avoid a potentially fatal mishap. Like all dogs, Greyhounds can swim, but the water level must be high enough so that they can climb out. A dog that is frightened may not be able to tread water for very long.

If you allow your Greyhound to run in a yard next to an in-ground pool, walk the dog over to the pool and make sure he understands that it contains water and is not a solid surface. This also applies to in-ground, indoor pools. One of our foster homes has an indoor lap pool, and a drenched Greyhound was very surprised when he discovered he couldn't walk on water! Fortunately his temporary owners were there to help him out.

Covered pools are no less of a hazard. People who are good swimmers have been known to drown in covered pools if they fall through; disorientation seems to set in almost immediately. The same applies to dogs, so make sure they understand that the cover is, at best, a flimsy surface and that water is underneath.

The best solution is to erect a fence around the pool and to keep that area off-limits to your dogs.

STAIRS

And now, for a match not made in heaven: Greyhounds and stairs. This is a tricky subject because dogs adapt to stairs in various ways. One thing is for certain, almost all of them exhibit some degree of trepidation. I believe there are two reasons for this. One is that stair-climbing is something new. The second reason has to do with their anatomy. Greyhounds are, quite obviously, very tall dogs. When you combine that with the highly developed muscles in their legs, you have an animal that bends somewhat differently from other dogs. He is built for flat-out racing, and the bulky leg muscles are something of a hindrance when it comes to steep inclines or declines. Also, the relatively short risers and narrow treads of most stairs make it very difficult for long-legged dogs.

Here's what you can do to make it easier for your dog. First of all, as was suggested for smooth floors, make the surface of your stairs as slip-free as possible. Get rubber or carpeted stair treads. Also, keep the stairs well lit, because it's always easier to accomplish anything when you can see what you're doing.

Alexandra is helped up the stairs.

If the stairs have open backs (risers), it is helpful to the dog if you enclose them, either with wood or with clear acrylic if you want to preserve the open look. I know of one dog whose leg slipped and was broken in open-backed stairs. It was painful for the dog as well as traumatic to both the dog and her owner.

Be gentle and patient with your dog. You may find his fear of stairs silly, but it's very serious to him. Whatever you do, don't force him. You may wind up traumatizing him and turning what could have been a simple training job into a major production.

It's ideal if there are two people available to coax him up the steps — preferably close to the wall for security. One person can gently tug on the leash while the other can gently push from behind. If you have to go it alone, assume the rear position. It's futile to attempt to pull the dog up the steps by his leash. It reminds me a lot of the days when I was adopting out wild burros rescued from the Grand Canyon and Death Valley by The Fund for Animals. Before we learned the right way to do it, we would often attempt to pull the burros into the van. Needless to say, we failed. The burro would simply sit down, and that was the end of it. It wasn't until we learned to wrap the lead rope behind the hind legs and inch him forward that we made any progress. I applied this principle to Greyhounds and, presto, it worked! Put one of your arms behind the dog's rear legs, just above the hock, and nudge him forward. To descend, repeat the process, taking great care not to push him down the steps.

Quite often the Greyhound will take the steps three or more at a time. That's okay — at least he's moving forward! Eventually he will learn that he can relax going up and down steps and will take them one at a time.

If you have narrow, winding or steep steps (I have all three) it's going to take longer for the dog to get acclimated. Again, just be patient. Once the dog realizes that he's missing out on some good times by not climbing steps, he'll make an extra effort. As always, when he is successful give him lots of praise.

GREYHOUNDS AND CHILDREN

Many people who adopt a Greyhound do so because the breed has a reputation for being good with children. Generally speaking, this is true. However, there are a few things about ex-racers and children that bear mentioning, as well as several rules of safety that parents must teach their children to follow with any breed of dog. Greyhounds are, on the whole, a gentle breed, but any dog that is a stranger to you and your family should be approached with caution.

Before I go into the specifics about Greyhounds and children, I urge you to reread the portion of Chapter Two, under the heading "How to Choose Your Ideal Greyhound," that deals with children (page 24). I cannot stress enough that, nine times out of ten, when a dog is returned to us because it either growled or snapped at a child, an adult was not supervising the interaction. Are you really willing to stay alert when the dog and the child are together? If you have more than one child, will you have the time and energy for this task? Again, I suggest you reconsider adopting *any* dog until your children are over the age of six and are better able to understand the meaning of the word "no" and the possible consequences of their actions.

If you have already adopted a dog and are preparing for the arrival of a new baby (especially if it is your first child), there are things you can do to get your Greyhound used to the change. Before your baby comes home from the hospital, try to bring home an article of his or her clothing so the dog can get used to the scent. Make sure you give your dog just as much, or nearly as much, attention as before the baby arrived. Make sure he associates the new baby with good things. Give him treats *only* when the baby is around. Take him with you when you take the baby out in the carriage. Try your best to make him feel that the new addition is a welcome change and does not mean he no longer matters to you. For an in-depth discussion of this topic, read one of the many books on the subject. I recommend one in particular, and it is listed in Appendix Five.

THEIR PAST AFFECTS THEIR PRESENT

One thing to remember about ex-racers is that although they are docile dogs, they have not had a great deal of experience with children. Whether you are choosing your own dog or one is being chosen for you, make sure the Greyhound you bring home is easygoing and friendly. A very shy or retiring dog is likely to be upset by the noise and erratic movements of children. Likewise, a dog that is too outgoing and active may knock over very small children or want to try to dominate them. What you want is a dog that will be thrilled by the sight of children and want to play with them. You want a calm dog, but not one that is so calm that he will be frightened or annoyed by loud noises. You also want an active dog but not one that sees playtime as a way to assert his superiority. It's a fine line, but the adoption group should be able to help you.

Once you get your dog home, keep in mind that everything is new to him. Allow him to ease into his new environment with as little pressure as possible. In other words, the demands on him should be few — even the demand that he be affectionate or playful. He has a lot to absorb, so take it easy on him and let him make the first move toward you and your children. In the beginning, your new Greyhound needs a lot of time out. Even a well-intentioned hug can be too much.

To the extent that your children are capable of understanding, try to impress on them that although they are excited to have a new dog in the house and have had a lot of time to prepare for him, the new dog was just thrust into the situation. Because of that, the dog is going to need time to feel like he's a member of the family. Reading to your children Chapter Three, "The Racing Life," which describes what the Greyhound's life was like on the track, should help them appreciate how strange living in a house must be to your dog.

LET SLEEPING DOGS LIE

One fact about track life that is especially pertinent to a Greyhound's new life as a companion is that at the track Greyhounds slept in crates. Because of that, they were never touched or disturbed in any way while they were asleep. To do so now might startle and frighten them, and it is possible that they could wake up and snap at the source of the disturbance. This is not due to any inherent viciousness, but, rather, it is more of a conditioned reflex. Both you and your children should learn to awaken the dog before touching him. Some Greyhounds have an odd habit of sleeping with their eyes half open. To the untutored eye it can look as if they are awake. The only way to tell the difference is to call the dog's name and see that he has responded and is really focusing on you. At that point, feel free to pet him, but even then, hugging him or standing over his bed in a way that seems threatening to him may be too much in the beginning.

CRATE ETIQUETTE

Another thing about track life that has bearing on a Greyhound's new life in a home is that in his previous life he had very few things of his own. The crate was one of them, and for this reason, some Greyhounds feel possessive of it. No child should ever go into a crate with any dog. It is not cute or charming, and it has the potential to end badly. Any dog, and especially one whose sole possession in life has been his crate, might feel either territorial or threatened in the confined space. Never allow a child to go into a crate, whether the dog is in it or not.

A dog bed can, in some cases, translate into a crate in the minds of some dogs. This is why leaning over a dog while he is on his bed, or hugging him, can be perceived as a threat. Certainly in the beginning it is best to restrict your affection to the dog to times when he is standing up, fully awake and in a receptive mood. You can read his body language to tell how he is feeling. If his tail is up and wagging, if he is smiling (not to be confused with the baring of teeth) or if he makes a move toward you with an open and pleasant expression on his face, then he is friendly and ready for a pat on the head or shoulder. Do not let your child hug a new Greyhound or any other strange dog. Hugs are commonly interpreted by dogs as dominant and threatening behavior.

DON'T LEAVE KIDS ALONE WITH DOGS

Children must always be supervised when interacting with the new dog. Do not allow them to be alone together — not even for "just a minute." In the few instances when I've received calls from people who have told me a Greyhound has snapped at their child, I always ask the same question: What was the child doing at the time? Often the answer has been that they didn't know — they weren't in the room. Children can provoke dogs, either accidentally or on purpose, just to see what the reaction will be. It is up to the parents or a responsible adult to supervise children's interaction with dogs. Keep children away from the dog's face, do not allow the dog to be hugged by them, do not allow them to taunt the dog (either physically or verbally) and, when you see that the dog is feeling tired or expressing in some way that he wants to be left alone, call for a time-out. Put the dog in his crate or have the children go into another room for awhile.

Most dogs, and especially Greyhounds, give warning signals before they are driven to retaliate. Do you notice that the dog leaves the room when the children enter? Does she retreat to her crate when the neighborhood children come to visit? The dog is telling you she is on sensory overload and does not wish to be disturbed. You, and your children, need to respect her privacy.

BE CAREFUL AFTER SURGERY OR AN INJURY

After being spayed or neutered, Greyhounds, like anyone who has just had major surgery, are especially tender and sensitive. Be sure they are given ample quiet time, that they are not handled excessively and that they are not allowed (or encouraged) to engage in boisterous play.

Some Greyhounds that were retired because of a leg injury, either a healing broken leg or a torn or pulled ligament or tendon, can still be sore. Make sure that your children know where the pain is and that they avoid the area. They must be careful neither to touch it nor to lean on it. A dog that is experiencing a sudden sharp pain might well snap at the source of the pain.

FOOD TIME IS PRIVATE TIME

Children must never be allowed to play near a dog's food bowl while the dog is eating. Likewise, children must never try to remove a piece of rawhide or a toy from a dog's mouth. I strongly discourage feeding bits of your food from the table while you are eating. It turns the dog into a beggar, and, if you have more than one dog, there can be a fight over which one gets the morsel. Your child's fingers or face could be caught in the middle.

KEEP DOORS AND FENCE GATES CLOSED

It must be impressed on children that Greyhounds can never be allowed to run loose in an unfenced area. Ideally the outside area around the door that is most often used in your house will

Alice and Ike are best buddies.

already be fenced. This is something that most adoption groups require. But if this is not the case in your home, then you must teach your children never to stand in a doorway with the door open. Maintain a policy of "Go in or go out, but close the door behind you." To prevent accidents, put up a gate in a hallway near a door to prevent the dog from darting out of an open door. It can also serve as a reminder to the children that Greyhounds cannot go out unleashed.

Remind children, too, to close outside fence gates as they enter or exit. A spring attached to the gate to pull it shut is a good back-up plan. Toddlers who are too young to understand the serious-ness of the situation can sometimes open a front door before you even know what's happening. A hook-and-eye latch placed above your child's reach will prevent such an accident. Another potential hazard exists in houses where an inside house door leads to the garage. If both the garage door and the house door are left open, the dog can escape that way. Again, be mindful of the potential for tragedy, stay alert and keep those doors and gates closed.

GREYHOUNDS AND KIDS CAN BE GREAT TOGETHER

Despite all of the above warnings, most Greyhounds and kids live together happily. When you are a child, nothing compares to having a dog as your very best friend. As adults, some of our fondest memories of growing up are of good times with the family dog. I am merely trying to prevent accidents from happening. That way you, your children and your new Greyhound can live happily ever after!

CREATING A SECURE ENVIRONMENT

The final piece of advice I have for acclimating your new addition to the family is to give him a special place of his own. He will have his crate, of course, and some people choose to make it available by leaving the door open long after the dog actually "needs" it. But eventually you will want him to get more into the swing of things. What often does the trick is his own soft dog bed or a plump comforter. He will soon recognize it as his own spot and become quite attached to it. From that vantage point he can watch his new family and figure out just where he's going to fit in.

CHOOSING THE BEST VETERINARIAN

There are a few other things you should do in advance of the dog's arrival. First of all, if you don't already have a veterinarian, now is a good time to interview some. Just because you have located a vet near you, or if you already have someone you have been using for years, does not mean he or she is the best choice for your new Greyhound. What you need is not just a good vet but a vet who is aware of the special nature and idiosyncrasies of Greyhounds. In addition, try to find a veterinarian who will refer you to a *board-certified* specialist should the need arise. Oftentimes you can save precious time, and money, by dealing with a specialist who has had more experience with certain disorders and who can diagnose and treat more reliably.

Call and ask if the veterinarian has other Greyhounds as clients. If not, what about other sighthounds (Afghans, Borzois

King relaxing in his bed.

and so on)? As you will learn in later chapters, sighthounds really are different, and you don't want to use a vet who is treating one for the first time. If possible, get the adoption center to recommend a good, qualified veterinarian in your area. Even if you have to drive a little farther, it's worth it to get a suitable doctor.

In addition to technical expertise, try to find a vet with whom you have a good rapport. He or she should be willing to answer all of your questions, take your concerns seriously and anticipate your dog's needs. If you question what experience he or she has had with Greyhounds, the vet should welcome it as a sign of your commitment to your dog rather than as an attack on his or her professionalism. Remember, you will be putting your dog's life in this person's hands.

I also recommend that you do some comparison shopping as to the vet's rates. One man who adopted a Greyhound from me recently was charged double what my vet charges just for a basic office visit! All tests and shots were extra, of course. Look for a veterinarian who is knowledgeable about sighthounds, has a humane outlook and offers good rates.

Even if your Greyhound comes to you spayed or neutered and fully inoculated, I suggest taking him to your veterinarian for a checkup. Most adoption kennels are overworked, and it is possible that yours did not have the time or the staff to give your dog a complete examination. Besides, it's a good idea for your vet to see your dog at least once when he is well, so that if he becomes ill, there will be a point of comparison.

Have your dog weighed, and get a routine examination of eyes, ears, heart, lungs and teeth. Have your dog tested for heartworm and the presence of the four most prevalent tick-borne diseases (Lyme, Rocky Mountain Spotted Fever, Ehrliciosis and Babesiosis) if this has not already been done. For a complete discussion of tick-borne diseases, please see Chapter Five, "Care and Feeding." If a fecal test has not been done recently, bring in a fresh stool sample.

If you have other pets, you would be wise to isolate your new Greyhound from them unless he has had all of his shots as well as a negative fecal test. The chance that he has an infectious disease is slim, but why risk it at all? Many racing kennels do not inoculate their dogs after the first year on the theory that since they are associating only with each other, they cannot pick up any illnesses. This, of course, is shortsighted. Some diseases, such as parvovirus, are airborne. Others, such as rabies, could be transmitted if a rabid raccoon somehow wandered into a kennel's turnout pen and bit a dog. On the East Coast in 1991 there was a virtual rabies epidemic, so it is essential that these dogs be protected immediately.

GET YOUR SUPPLIES IN ADVANCE

Finally, before your dog arrives, get a supply of food, feeding and water bowls, a collar and leash (if they are not provided), a crate and a soft bed. You can also purchase an identification tag for your new dog in advance. It doesn't matter if you don't know yet what you are going to name him. The important information on the tag is your name, address and phone number. If the worst happened and your new dog was lost within a few days of his arrival, he would be in double trouble. He would not only be unfamiliar with you and your neighborhood, he would also be unfamiliar with life outside the track. Even if the adoption group puts one of their tags on your dog, you need one with your own vital statistics. That way if your dog runs off and winds up at a house around the corner, the people can contact you directly and the return will be made that much easier and quicker.

Once you have all of your supplies, you can bring your dog into his new environment and spend your time getting to know him rather than dashing out to go shopping. There's no sense letting anything interfere with the wonderful adventure you two are about to embark on together.

Chapter Five

Care and Feeding

*I*n Chapter Three, we discussed the importance of a good diet for a racing dog. However, since your dog is no longer a professional athlete, what should he be fed now? First, let's examine exactly what racing dogs are fed at the track. The idea here, of course, is not to duplicate it but, rather, to diverge gradually from that regimen. If you change your dog's diet too quickly, he is likely to experience anything from mild gastric disturbances (such as gas) to diarrhea.

THE TRACK DIET

The emphasis at the racetrack is on performance, and in order to foster it, racing Greyhounds are fed a high-protein, high-carbohydrate diet. Protein, of course, is good for muscle development, and carbohydrates provide energy for the long haul.

Compared to other dog breeds, Greyhounds at the track are fed enormous quantities of food. Because they burn off so many calories during a race, it would be easy for them to lose a lot of weight. The trainers compensate by feeding them more than most dogs their size eat. Typically, both the males and females are fed two pounds a day.

Each kennel has its own recipe, but the basics always include raw beef mixed with a high-protein dry food. Added to that can be vegetables (often spinach or turnip greens for extra iron), corn oil (for the coat), salt (to replace what is lost during a race), water (to compensate for the extra salt), powdered vitamins and electrolytes. Bowls of water are kept filled in each crate.

INTRODUCING NEW FOOD

The first item you can omit from your dog's new diet is raw meat. Not only can it be rather unpleasant to deal with, but also he doesn't need it. Raw meat can also be the source of food poisoning, including the potentially deadly *E. coli* bacteria.

If you want him to have meat, substitute a good, high-quality canned dog food that doesn't contain meat by-products. If you knew what those by-products really were, you'd never feed them to your dog. Incidentally, dogs can get by quite well on dry dog food alone. It is, after all, nutritionally balanced. However, I recommend making additions to it in part for variety and in part for added nutrition. Greyhounds just off of the track have never been given dry kibble alone, so don't be surprised if in the beginning they don't really know what to do with it. Many seem to view it as a bowl of cereal without the milk!

If you are only feeding dry food, start with four cups per day for the females and five cups per day for the males (half in the morning, half in the evening), see how your dog's weight responds and adjust accordingly. Feeding your dog twice a day is important because although he can survive on a once-a-day feeding plan, it puts a much greater burden on his digestive tract. Once-a-day feedings were developed for the convenience of people, but it does not do your dog much of a favor. Dogs fed once a day also are more likely to beg and may become tense or irritable due to low blood sugar.

Since your dog is no longer racing, you should downgrade from a high-protein dry dog food to one that is designed for normal adult maintenance. When your dog reaches the age of seven, you might want to consider a lower-fat or lower-protein food formulated for the "mature" dog.

You Get What You Pay For

Whatever your dog's age, you should go for a high-quality food for a number of reasons. One, the quality brands are often concentrated, which means you don't have to feed as much. Two, they aren't loaded with fillers or the dreaded "meat by-products."

Three, good dry dog food tends to harden the stool, making your clean-up job a lot easier. Four, it is also better for teeth than soft foods or meat alone. And, finally, you will be giving your dog the best ingredients, which, in turn, will keep your dog healthier.

I never recommend giving your dog the individually wrapped burger-type semi-moist foods. Not only are they filled with salt, sugar and artificial coloring, but they offer little more than empty calories. They will promote bad teeth, indigestion and obesity.

As for which brand to use, I recommend trying several kinds and seeing how your dog fares. I started off using one well-known premium brand until I discovered that it was giving several of my dogs gas. I switched brands, and the gas never came back. Yet, other people I know use that particular brand, and their dogs are just fine. The point is, each dog's metabolism is different, just as every person's is. Despite some people's almost fanatical allegiance to one brand of dog food, in truth, there is no one food that is perfect for every dog. Experiment to see which yours likes and which agrees with him. Be careful, however, not to switch foods abruptly. Blend in the old brand with the new gradually over the course of a week. Abrupt changes can cause diarrhea.

CONTINUE WITH VEGETABLES

I am very much in favor of continuing the track's practice of giving Greyhounds vegetables. Dogs are omnivores, not carnivores. What this means is that in the wild, dogs do not eat only meat (as do cats). Dogs eat grasses and other greens, and I believe we do them a great disservice by limiting their diet to meat.

If cooking vegetables is too much for you, try the canned varieties. My dogs are fond of all vegetables, but especially carrots, spinach, stewed tomatoes and cauliflower. Avoid potatoes (unless they are mashed) as well as corn, since most dogs have trouble digesting them.

Scraps from your plate are also good, not as a substitute for a balanced canine diet, but as a supplement. Cooked rice (white or brown) is also a nice addition to his diet and can be helpful in firming up loose stools.

COOKING FOR YOUR DOG

There are three reasons why I cook for my dogs: I enjoy it, I believe it gives them added vitamins and other nutrients and I know it adds variety to their life. I am not suggesting that you substitute a homemade diet for commercially prepared dry food. However, I am suggesting this as an addition to dry food, which should form the basis of their diet.

To cut down on preparation time, I cook for my dogs twice a week and simply dole out refrigerated portions (reheated, of course). I change vegetables often and always combine at least two, such as carrots and spinach. I also cook up a big batch of rice or noodles, and to that I add either well-drained, cooked ground beef or boiled chicken. The mixture can get a little dry, so I add either beef or chicken broth. The consistency should not be that of soup, but more of a stew. At feeding time, twice a day, I give them a cup or so of the stew well mixed with their dry food. The males, which are larger, get two cups of dry food, while the females get one cup. As an added treat, every now and then I add a heaping tablespoon of low-fat cottage cheese or a small piece of cheese on top as a garnish and to provide a little extra calcium. To say that they love it is an understatement.

There are a few staples that you can have on hand to add to your dog's food that do not require a lot of work. I am rarely without a container of cottage cheese, a can of mixed vegetable juice, a jar of wheat germ, various cans of vegetables and, of course, some sort of cooked grain (rice, barley, millet and so on). Incidentally, if you plan to feed dry food only, the mixed vegetable juice does wonders for it as does a light sprinkle of grated cheese.

THE PROS AND CONS OF OIL

I would add oil to a dog's food only if his coat looked dry. Otherwise you are simply adding empty calories to your dog's food, and all that extra fat is no better for your dog than it is for you. Also, if your dog has a tendency toward loose stools, as may well be the case in the beginning, omit the oil, as it will only aggravate the condition. If you ever need to add oil for a dry coat, the best kind to get is one high in essential fatty acids. These are generally found in fish oils (cod liver oil, for example) and provide the most complete nutrition and absorption. A few teaspoons a day will do until the coat is back in shape. A lot of all-purpose oil that people add to their dog's food simply passes through the animal's system without doing any real good.

FOOD SUPPLEMENTS

Once the dog is finished racing, electrolytes can be omitted from his diet. Vitamins, however, are a different story. If you take vitamins yourself, you may want to give them to your dog, too. But if the food your dog is getting says "nutritionally complete" on the label (and it should), then extra vitamins may be unnecessary. On the other hand, if you are anything like me, you may want to give your dog vitamins just for good measure. It is generally a good idea to give balanced canine multivitamins as opposed to adding specific ones. Such a practice may add too much of a particular nutrient. My current practice involves blending a powder containing trace minerals and vitamins into the dogs' food. I do this because these particular nutrients are hard to get in any diet — human or canine.

Glucosamine and chondroitin are two other popular supplements said to increase glycosaminoglycans in the joints, provide connective tissue support, reduce inflammation and aid in flexibility. If you choose to add these to your dog's diet, determine first if your dog has arthritis or other inflammatory joint problems. If the dog's stiffness is from another cause (nerve damage, for example), then no amount of additives will help and you will be wasting your money.

HOW MUCH IS ENOUGH?

Many dogs that are just off the track need a little fattening up. Most people love this process, and so do the dogs. Be careful, though, not to give them too much of a good thing. Greyhounds are lean by nature, and overweight ones can develop joint trouble or arthritis from carrying around more pounds than their frame can handle. A good rule of thumb is that you should be able to feel your Greyhound's ribs easily, but you should not be able to see the outline of them.

In the case of convalescing dogs that need to be coaxed into eating, my theory, which is backed up by veterinarians, is that you do whatever it takes to get something into them. I've found that canned cat food is irresistible. Beef tea, a broth made from round steak, is also quite tempting and is helpful if the dog cannot, or will not, eat solid food. Other delicacies include rice pudding and jarred baby food. One of my elderly Afghan Hounds, Seamus, made a comeback from pneumonia with a diet of toasted ham and cheese sandwiches! Hiding his antibiotics in the melted cheese was also a convenient method of getting the pills down his throat. Please understand that this is not meant to be a full-time diet. But when a dog is extremely ill and it is either junk food or no food, go with the junk. Just make sure they don't get spoiled and want it for the rest of their lives!

When you bring your new Greyhound home, don't try switching brands of food every week. Try a particular diet for a few weeks, and see how it goes. Gas or diarrhea at the beginning may just be a reaction to new food, new water, a new schedule and general stress. In fact, just by switching brands too often and too quickly you may create the very problems (gas and/or diarrhea) that you are trying to avoid.

Because Greyhounds are so tall, it is helpful to them if you feed them on an elevated platform. That way they don't have to gulp their food or stretch their necks too far to get at their dish. This is especially important for older dogs as, with age, a dog's trachea is not as flexible as it once was. An older dog is much more likely to choke or gag on his food if he has to reach down for it. Keep dog bowls elevated 12 to 16 inches from the floor, depending on the height of the dog. By the way, stainless steel or ceramic bowls are the best because you can sterilize them and keep them free of bacteria. Stainless steel bowls have the edge because they are lighter weight and if you drop them, they won't break. Plastic bowls cannot tolerate the high heat required to kill off germs.

WATER, WATER EVERYWHERE

Veteran horse trainer George Millar once told me that water was the cheapest medicine. He was right, of course, and no living creature, dogs included, should ever go thirsty. Water flushes the system, keeps the kidneys in good working order and aids in digestion. Keep the water bowl filled, and make sure you scrub it out on a regular basis.

SPAYING AND NEUTERING

Your visit to the vet is a good time to set up an appointment for the dog to be spayed or neutered if it hasn't been done already. It cannot be overemphasized how important this is. With tens of thousands of Greyhounds, and over 13 million other dogs, dying every year for the want of a home, one would have to be either incredibly naïve or thoughtless to even consider bringing another Greyhound litter into the world. Don't forget that 30 percent of the dogs that wind up in shelters are purebred. No matter how beautiful or talented or good-natured your dog is, there are hundreds more just as good, or even better. So don't think that by breeding your dog you will be creating more "perfect" specimens. Other perfect specimens of all kinds already exist, and they are dying by the millions!

As for breeding ex-racers to other breeds of dogs, or to AKC Greyhounds, forget that too. The bottom line with all breeding is that there are already more dogs (and cats) in the world than there are homes for them. Even if you think you will find good homes for all of the puppies you create, what about the puppies' puppies? And their puppies? And what about the homes you have "taken up" because you chose to breed your dog? You can be sure that other deserving dogs already alive will now die because there is no room for them.

And, if you think that your dog will never be bred because you are just too careful, bear in mind that most mixed-breed dogs are the result of accidental matings. The sexual urge is very strong when a female is in heat and a male is on her trail. Dogs have been known to move heaven and earth to get at the object of their affection. It only takes a moment's inattention from you and it could be too late.

HEALTH ADVANTAGES .

The health advantages to spaying and neutering are considerable. Male dogs that have not been neutered are prone to testicular cancer in their older years as well as prostate trouble. Uterine cancer and mammary tumors are common in unspayed females, as is pyrometra, an infection of the uterus that can be fatal if not treated promptly. I have been asked why these diseases do not kill dogs in the wild, and the answer is that in some cases they do. However, because wild dogs are sexually and reproductively active, the various organs are kept in good shape. By contrast, a domestic, unneutered male dog that is constantly stimulated by the odor of females in heat, but that never has the chance to breed, can develop chronic inflammations. Likewise, unspayed females that regularly go into heat but are never bred are also prone to problems. It really is more humane, from many standpoints, to spay and neuter, and many adoption groups have this surgery performed on Greyhounds before they enter their new home.

GROOMING

In general, Greyhounds are very clean and do not need a tremendous amount of care. That does not mean, however, that they should only be bathed once a year whether they need it or not. Grooming allows you to spend quality time with your dog, increases the bond between you and gives you the opportunity to head off potential health problems before they become serious.

If your dog comes to you with fleas, a nontoxic flea bath is in order right away. (See Chapter Six for specific recommendations concerning flea prevention.) The presence of fleas almost surely means the dog has tapeworm, so it would be wise to be on the lookout for telltale rice-like segments in his stools. Otherwise, a

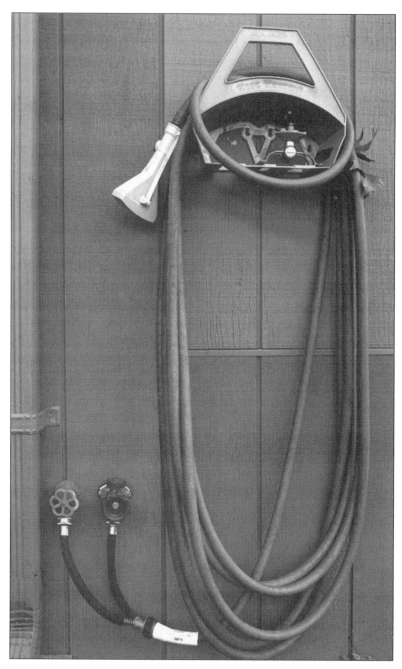

A plumber can easily install hot and cold running water outside.

bath every six to eight weeks helps remove dead hair and keeps him smelling fresh. Always use a shampoo made specifically for dogs. Human shampoo will dry out a dog's skin even with only one washing because the pH balance of dog skin is different from ours.

The Best Way to Bathe Your Dog

Do not bathe your dog in cold water. Even on the hottest summer day, a Greyhound can become deeply chilled by the icy water of a garden hose. It is a very simple matter for a plumber to install hot and cold faucets on your outside water spigot. Then you can attach a U-shaped hose that connects to both faucets and attach that to a regular hose. Just blend the hot with the cold until you've reached a comfortable temperature. The cool side of room temperature should be fine.

The ideal way to bathe your dog is in a tub at your waist level. That way you won't strain your back bending over and you'll be able to get a better look at the dog. If this is not possible, your

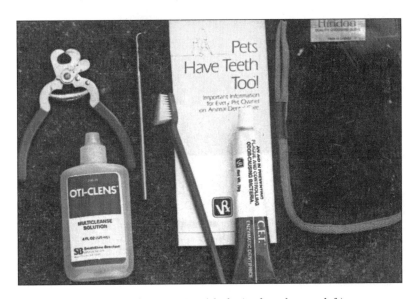

Some items for grooming (clockwise from bottom left):
ear cleaning solution, toenail trimmers, tooth scaler,
canine toothbrush and toothpaste and grooming glove.

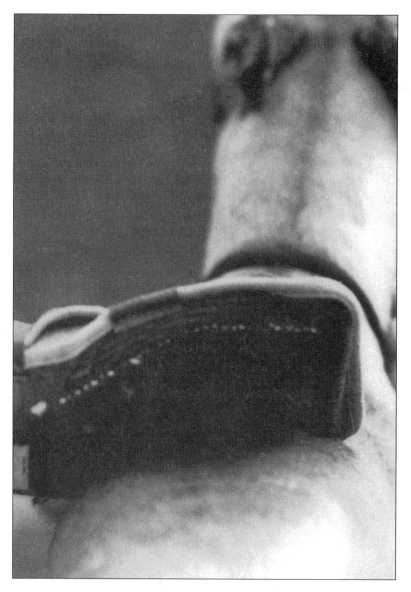

Grooming the coat with the hound glove.

regular tub will do. You may want to have someone hold the dog, or you can simply tie his leash to the water faucets so that he can stand comfortably but cannot escape. Be sure to provide a non-slip surface on the bottom of the tub.

You should get a device for the faucet that acts as a shower or spray, if you don't have one, then fill a plastic bowl (*not* glass, please) with warm water. Plug the dog's ears with cotton, and wet him thoroughly. Next, shampoo, taking care to avoid the eyes and mouth. Rinse thoroughly (shampoo residue can cause flaking skin), repeat as necessary, and you're done. Most Greyhounds will stand quietly for all of this even if they aren't crazy about it! Always dry your dog completely, and, in cold weather, keep him out of drafts and do not allow him outside for several hours after the bath.

While you are bathing him, check his ears for dirt and ticks. If you see dirt, wipe it out with a cotton ball, not a cotton swab. If the dirt has a foul odor or is very thick, he may have an ear infection, so see your veterinarian. Check toenail length at bath time, too.

Finally, brush the coat daily with a flat rubber or sisal glove (called, appropriately enough, a hound glove) or a fine-tooth comb. Most Greyhounds love being brushed and practically purr with delight. You might try a little muscle massage at the same time. You'll soon discover that grooming will become the highlight of the day for both of you.

SPECIAL HEALTH ISSUES

The vast majority of Greyhounds are, as a breed, unusually healthy. They have, after all, managed to survive for over 8,000 years and most of them make their living as professional athletes in their early years. You and your veterinarian may be very well-versed in dog care in general, but there are some health concerns, and idiosyncrasies, of the Greyhound breed that are worth noting.

A LITTLE KNOWLEDGE IS A DANGEROUS THING

Before I go any further, it is important that before you accept any layperson's advice (someone in a chat room, someone from your adoption group, etc.) on something as vital as the health care of your dog, consider the source: What are the credentials of the person giving the advice? Do they have any scientific training? Have they conducted a study using the scientific method? Has their study been subject to the all-important peer review? Are they basing their conclusions on a wide enough population? Are they basing their conclusions solely on observation, anecdotal evidence or hearsay? Are they basing their conclusions on the scientific studies of others? Do they have a vested interest in their conclusions (are they selling products or services based on their "evidence")? Did they first come to a conclusion (a bias) and then looked for agreement in their observations?

Remember, even the ancient Greek philosopher Aristotle, who taught us so much about science, drew many false conclusions because he based them on what he regarded as common sense rather than on experiments. An accurate conclusion can be reached only when deductive reasoning is used in combination with inductive reasoning.

THYROID TESTING

After a few months, when your Greyhound's new routine is well established, it may be a good time to reassess his overall health. One thing you may want to check is his thyroid level. Classic symptoms of hypothyroidism (underactive thyroid) include lethargy, listlessness, a reddish-brown tinge to the fur, a uniformly sparse coat that is also dry and brittle and thick, puffy, darkly pigmented skin. *True hypothyroidism in dogs of any breed is uncommon and affects less than 1 percent of dogs.*

First off, I want to clear up some misinformation that has been circulating in the Greyhound world. Some people in the adoption community who perhaps mean well but who have neither the knowledge nor the credentials, have been, in effect, prescribing medication for animals. I am referring to the erroneous notion that Greyhounds, as a group, suffer from hypothyroidism. So insidious is this fallacy that one of the largest animal blood-testing laboratories in the country, Antech, sent out a special bulletin to veterinarians warning them that some adoption groups are wrongly urging their members to put their Greyhounds on supplements. In some places thyroid supplementation is being touted as a "cure" for everything from social anxieties such as shyness and thunderstorm phobia, to the typical thigh baldness that we see on dogs newly off the track. Sadly, some owners are heeding this bad advice and are giving supplements to Greyhounds who may not need it — and may be endangering their dogs in the process.

The endocrine system, of which the thyroid is a part, is complex and not wholly understood — even by those who have studied it for years. The thyroid gland controls the body's metabolism and secretes either more or less hormones into the bloodstream, depending on energy demands. If a dog (or person) is diagnosed as hypothyroid, it means their thyroid is not secreting the appropriate amount of hormones that the body needs.

Many members of the sighthound family, including Greyhounds, have thyroid levels that are normal for them but which are lower than most other breeds. In other words, what is normal for a Poodle (or most other breeds) is not normal for a Greyhound. Therefore, if you mistakenly assume that the Greyhound should have the same thyroid level as a Poodle, you will be trying to correct a deficiency that does not exist. Once again, it is important to remember that, as athletes, Greyhounds need less of a metabolism boost than do other dogs. Unnecessary thyroid supplementation will cause the Greyhound's thyroid gland to stop functioning and to become dependent on the medication. Incidentally, once the thyroid is "turned off" it will never function again, even if the supplementation is later withdrawn. Some consequences of "pumping up" the Greyhound's system unnaturally are that it can cause an elevated heart rate, worsen existing heart conditions, create disturbances in eye movement and can even lead to premature death.

Many factors influence the thyroid level in the body, and a simple T4 test, which is what some people recommend, does not present a full enough profile to determine if a dog of any breed really is hypothyroid. Thyroid levels are affected by stress, medication and even other diseases. On top of that some of the tests themselves have certain limitations. It is for these reasons that you must proceed with caution.

The first step is to observe if a dog has any or all of the classic symptoms I've already mentioned. If so, the next move is to run a three-part blood work panel that will test the levels of T3, T4 and the TSH response (thyroid stimulating hormone). Should these figures point to clinical hypothyroidism *for a Greyhound,* then a further panel can be sent to a lab, which will check on the following: Total Thyroxine (TT4), Total Triiodothyronine (TT3), Free (unbound) T4 (FT4), Free (unbound) T3 (FT3), T4 autoantibody, T3 autoantibody, Thyroid Stimulating Hormone and Thyroglobulin autoantibody. At present, the Diagnostic Laboratory at Michigan State University is known nationally as setting the standard for offering extremely accurate and reliable results.

Do any Greyhounds have an underactive thyroid? Probably the number who do is in the range of the overall percentage of dogs who have it. But giving a dog thyroid supplementation is not to be considered unless classic symptoms are present and extensive panels of tests provide irrefutable proof of its need. For a further discussion of this subject, please read the scientific documentation referenced in Appendix Three of this book.

LOWER WHITE BLOOD COUNT (WBC)/HIGHER PACKED CELL VOLUME (PCV)

Another area in which Greyhounds differ physiologically from other breeds has to do with their blood. If you keep in mind that Greyhounds are athletes, then it makes sense that their blood will have more red blood cells (which carry oxygen) and fewer white blood cells. Some veterinarians are not aware of this difference and, upon seeing lower white blood cells and higher packed cell volume, draw the wrong conclusion and recommend subjecting Greyhounds to painful, and costly, bone marrow aspirates while they search in vain for a problem that does not exist. Assuming your Greyhound appears healthy otherwise, then before you agree to such a procedure, I recommend that you, or your veterinarian, read the scientific documentation referenced in Appendix Three of this book.

Tick-Borne Diseases

One of the sad facts of life for Greyhounds in racing kennels is that they do not always receive the best care. One manifestation of this is ticks, the not-so-harmless pests that can transmit deadly diseases.

No national records are being kept on Greyhounds and ticks, but according to Dr. Cynthia Holland, a microbiologist and director of the ProtaTek Reference Laboratory in Chandler, Arizona, since 1995 approximately 40 percent of the Greyhounds she has tested, literally thousands of dogs, are asymptomatic carriers of one or more tick-borne disease agents.

More times than I care to remember, we have received ex-racers just off the track that had literally hundreds of ticks attached to their bodies. It takes several volunteers with tweezers an hour to get them clean. The problem is that although the ticks are removed, the damage that they may have inflicted could be just beginning.

While the symptoms of some tick-borne diseases show up almost immediately, others may lie dormant for years. By then, a dog's owner may well have forgotten that the dog was tick-infested at one time. And, of course, once the disease has reached the chronic phase, it is not only more difficult to treat but more costly as well.

Another problem with tick-borne diseases is that the symptoms can mimic other diseases, which is why they are known as The Great Impostors. For example, lethargy, lameness, seizures, a low platelet count or kidney failure could all be the signs of something other than a tick-borne disease. It is helpful to have a veterinarian who is willing to consider ticks as the culprit.

Yet another aspect of the Greyhound and tick problem is that because Greyhounds travel from track to track, it is highly possible for them to have picked up a tick in one location and taken it with them to an area where such a tick is not native. It is not uncommon, for example, for a Greyhound to be born in Kansas, trained in Arizona, raced in Florida and to wind up in Connecticut. From there he could be adopted by a family in New

Jersey. Not many vets in New Jersey are on the lookout for signs of babesiosis because it is almost unheard of in the state. Likewise, most vets in California are not alert to the dangers of Lyme disease in a dog. What you need to do is explain to your veterinarian that although your Greyhound may now be living in a particular locale, he could have been anywhere and exposed to any number of ticks.

The most common tick-borne diseases are Lyme disease, Rocky Mountain spotted fever, ehrlichiosis and babesiosis. When you adopt a Greyhound, ask if the dog had ticks. If so, get him tested. Find out, too, if the dog was ever given a Lyme disease vaccine. If so, when your dog is tested, the titer results will be elevated. Make sure you ask your veterinarian for a panel that will test for all four diseases. If you are questioned, explain how the dog has spent much of his life on the road.

Once the results come in, treatment is a little tricky. There are some veterinarians who do not believe in treating a dog until he shows symptoms. Others rely solely on test results, symptoms or not.

If the results are negative, you may want to consider getting a Lyme vaccine for your Greyhound if you live in a region affected by the disease. Some veterinarians recommend it routinely, while others say that it is only partially effective and that some evidence suggests that the vaccine itself can compromise a dog's immune system. It is worth noting that similar research to that involved in coming up with the Lyme vaccine for dogs was also used in developing one for humans, and that vaccine has now been withdrawn from the market.

If the result is positive and the decision is to treat, doxycycline is the drug of choice for Rocky Mountain, Lyme and ehrlichia. The usual dosage is 500 milligrams twice a day for four weeks. Too short a course or too weak a dose may actually do more harm than good, as it can kill off the weaker bacteria and allow the stronger to thrive. Babesia require the use of either the antibiotic Clindamycin or a drug called imidocarb diproprionate. The latter is not yet approved by the FDA, and its use necessitates a special license which not many veterinarians have. Although it is the most effective weapon against babesia, it can also produce severe side effects. A new form of imidocarb diproprionate called IMIZOL© is also an alternative for treating babesia. It is in a sterile solution and is given in two doses, two weeks apart.

Yet another variable involves dogs whose results are borderline. To treat or not to treat? Some vets do; some don't. Certainly, by treating a dog, you will greatly reduce the chances of damage. On the other hand, overuse and misuse of antibiotics, both in humans and in animals, has caused some strains of bacteria to become resistant. If your dog is borderline but not showing symptoms, one course of action might be to wait for six months and retest. If the titer is the same, it probably means that the dog was exposed at some point in his life but that he has fought off the infection.

Combine your intuition with the experience of your veterinarian. A second opinion, or a conversation with a microbiologist at the testing laboratory, may be in order.

By the way, a new heartworm test (called the SNAP test) can reveal exposure to Lyme, RMSF and ehrlichia in dogs, but it is not a substitute for an in-depth tick panel, because it cannot reveal active infection. In other words, negative is negative, but positive may mean only that the dog has been exposed to the disease and may not have an active infection.

While all of the above may sound rather grim, bear in mind that except for the most advanced cases, tick-borne diseases are treatable. The key is to test your dog to determine if he is infected, to treat him if he is, and to prevent any further infections. In Chapter Six, I will discuss what types of tick preventatives are safe for Greyhounds.

PANNUS (UBERREITER'S DISEASE)

Pannus is a progressive disease of the eye that is seen in some Greyhounds. It is characterized by overgrowth of the blood vessels on the whites of the eyes that give them a red appearance, a clouding of the eye, a thickening of the third eyelid, and in advanced cases, ulcers on the cornea. There is no cure, and in time, it can lead to blindness. However, a simple, inexpensive treatment (which must be given lifelong) can keep the disease in remission. Assuming that your dog's eyes are not ulcerated, she can be treated with prednisolone acetate eye drops, which are given once a day and cost about $15 for a six-week supply.

Osteosarcoma (Bone Cancer)

Osteosarcoma is seen in some Greyhounds because it is a disease that is more common in long-limbed dogs. At present, of all breeds, Rottweilers have the highest rate of the disease. Bone cancer is not limited to the legs however, and can affect any bone in the body (ribs, jaw, skull, etc.). If you notice that your dog is limping, even intermittently, and you are not aware of any recent or old injury, it might be wise to have your veterinarian X-ray the area.

If the result is positive, there is no cure. Assuming the disease has not yet spread to the lungs, you have the choice of keeping the dog comfortable with pain relief, or, if the cancer is in a suitable location, amputating. If you choose amputation, do not consider surgery unless it is accompanied by chemotherapy. My experience has been that both surgery and chemotherapy are best handled by board-certified veterinary surgeons and oncologists, since they have vastly more experience and training. You will need to ask your veterinarian for a referral to a specialist.

One other thing to consider: While this is admittedly not a scientific sampling, I have placed more than 4,000 Greyhounds over the years. Of the dogs I know of who have been diagnosed with bone cancer, the survival rate with or without surgery or amputation is about the same — six to eight months. I have known some who were simply kept comfortable on pain medication who lived over a year, and I have known others who died on the operating table. Before choosing either alternative, think carefully about your dog's age and temperament (how close is she to the end of a Greyhound's normal life span of 12 to 14 years? how accepting is she of changes in her life?), her quality of life (will this be a life worth living?), and your ability, both financially and emotionally, to care for her (consider the monetary costs and the stress on yourself).

As with any major health decision, always ask yourself what your real motivation is for the treatment. Are you doing this for the dog's benefit, or because you cannot face losing him? In some cases, it might be a kindness to the dog not to put him through painful procedures that have very uncertain outcomes.

LARYNGEAL PARALYSIS (PARALYZED LARYNX)

Laryngeal paralysis is a progressive disorder that decreases the ability of the nerves in the throat to control the muscles that open and close the larynx. Initially, it is characterized by one or more of the following: coughing, panting, intolerance to heat, intolerance to moderate exercise, gagging and a hoarse-sounding bark. In the final stages, the dog will have increased difficulty swallowing and breathing, and, if left untreated, will die a very painful death.

When my Ajax was 11 years old he began exhibiting such symptoms. In vain, I consulted four different general practice veterinarians, each of whom offered a different opinion: anxiety, allergies, "old dog lung" and the last veterinarian had no idea at all! Finally, I consulted a board-certified veterinary internist. Ajax was diagnosed within minutes and, on his 13th birthday, had the only treatment available for this life-threatening condition: laryngeal tie-back surgery.

The procedure involves cutting a flap on one side of the throat and tying back the muscles that control the larynx so that side is permanently open. Dogs quickly learn how to swallow and, for most, the problem is solved. The down side is that it leaves the dog vulnerable to aspiration pneumonia, which can occur if the dog accidentally inhales either food or water or vomit and it goes into his lungs instead of down his esophagus. Given that there is no other treatment for the condition, it is a risk worth taking. To help prevent inhalation of food and water, an elevated food bowl is a must after this surgery. By the way, my Afghan Hound Padillac had the same problem and, like Ajax, survived the surgery and continues to thrive.

DENTAL CARE

Most dogs that are just off the track have terrible-looking teeth that are covered with tartar. More than one veterinarian has looked skeptical when told that a certain dog was only two or three when what he or she saw looked more like the mouth of a 10-year-old. The reason is that racing dogs have a totally soft diet, so the tartar builds quickly. Also, many gnaw on their crates out of boredom and wear their teeth down.

Get your dog's teeth cleaned regularly by a veterinarian to prevent tooth loss and gum infection. This can be done initially while the dog is being spayed or neutered so that he has to be anesthetized only once. I cannot stress enough how important it is to keep your dog's teeth clean. Not only is the odor from dirty teeth offensive but, more important, decayed teeth or infected gums can jeopardize your dog's life. Bacteria from mouth infections have a tendency to lodge in the valves of the heart, making them less able to operate properly. A dog can actually die from heart trouble brought on by bad teeth!

To maintain clean teeth, brush your dog's teeth weekly with special dog toothpaste. Your veterinarian will have it available as do pet supply catalogs. Also, hard dog biscuits or sterilized cow hooves help keep dogs' teeth clean, and dogs really love giving them a workout! Many people also give their dogs raw carrots to gnaw on. That way the dogs clean their teeth, massage their gums and get their vitamins all at once!

If you want to get really adventurous, you can try scaling your dog's teeth yourself. Dental tools are available in many pet supply stores. Start at the gum line and gently move the tool back and forth, gradually working your way toward the tip of the tooth. It takes patience, both on the part of the person and the dog, but it can avoid a yearly trip to the veterinarian's office for dentistry. Before you try this, however, you might want to ask your veterinarian to demonstrate the correct technique. If you use too much pressure you could damage the enamel on your dog's teeth. If a dog's teeth have considerable tartar, do not attempt to scale them

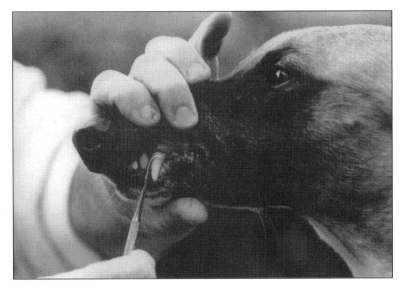

Sophie's teeth are scaled to remove tartar.

as you may succeed only in doing what you want to avoid, pushing the bacteria up under the gums.

There is a new dental product on the market that seems promising. It works by coating newly cleaned teeth with a slippery, nontoxic substance that makes it harder for tartar to form. Another product that may be of benefit is added to the dog's drinking water to reduce the amount of bacteria in his mouth.

ASSISTING THE OLDER DOG

A word about the older Greyhound: As with people, a dog's senses become weaker as he ages. Age comes on so gradually that many owners fail to notice that their old friend is not responding the way he used to. Impaired sight or hearing loss puts a dog at a disadvantage. It does not, however, have to mean the end.

I have had the pleasure of sharing my life with many older dogs, and, in fact, several of my dogs were over 10 when I adopted them. I sometimes joke that a dog doesn't start to get good until he's at least five! The point is that older dogs have a lot to give, and whatever small sacrifices we have to make to accommodate their needs are well worth it.

FEEDING

Older dogs sometimes develop a more selective appetite. Do not assume they are simply becoming spoiled. Perhaps their teeth are bothering them, perhaps they have developed a sensitive stomach, perhaps standing long enough to eat has become a problem. You cannot allow them to miss many meals before you take action. Of course, a visit to the vet is the first order of business. Once you have discovered the cause of the appetite loss, follow your vet's instructions. Ask, however, if certain additions to the diet might not be in order. When my elderly Fiona was suffering from kidney disease and it began to affect her appetite, I started off each morning by giving her a bottle of meat-based baby food, to which I added (on her internist's advice) an over-the-counter acid reducer. In his extreme old age, Ajax grew to depend on cans of the prescription diet A/D, which is formulated for convalescing dogs and has a very high calorie, vitamin and mineral content. When all else fails, few older dogs can resist the special attention involved in hand-feeding!

ELEVATE THE FOOD BOWL

As a dog ages, his trachea becomes less flexible. This can lead to choking and gagging problems, especially if he has to strain to reach down to floor level for his food. Elevating his dish will help enormously.

EYESIGHT AND HEARING

With age, a dog's eyesight can be diminished either by cataracts or by rods that were damaged earlier in life. Such dogs compensate by relying more and more on their sense of smell. Try to keep your furniture in the same place and always leave a nightlight on for them. Keep in mind that very bright sunlight can also be troublesome for older dogs with poor eyesight.

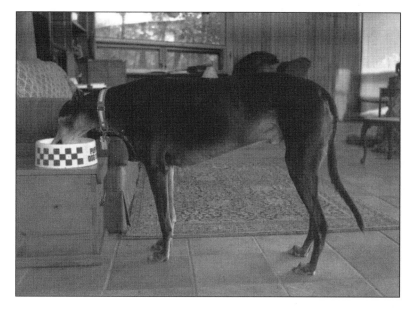

Older dogs especially appreciate elevated food bowls.

If your dog's hearing should start to fail, have patience, keep him out of harm's way by alerting him to dangers that he may not be able to hear coming and use a gentle touch to get his attention.

BLADDER CONTROL

Imperfect bladder control can also be a part of aging. Long ago I removed all of the wall-to-wall carpeting in my house and replaced it with ceramic tile. If an accident happens it is a simple matter for me to mop it up. Likewise, dog beds should have a plastic-covered foam pad inside with a soft cover outside that can be removed for easy washing. Don't fear that your house will look stark or barren. A few washable or dry-cleanable area rugs can do a lot to soften the overall effect.

Some older, spayed females become afflicted with a hormonal imbalance that causes them to become incontinent. If your previously housebroken girl is now dribbling, or outright urinating in her sleep, ask your veterinarian to run a test. If it comes back positive, a lifetime daily dose of the inexpensive drug phenylpropanolamine hydrochloride may solve the problem.

Greyhounds love to be stroked.

ARTHRITIS

Dogs, like people, are prone to arthritis as they age. This is especially true of ex-racers if they had broken bones that perhaps were set imperfectly or not at all. The good news is that nonsteroidal anti-inflammatory drugs (NSAIDs) that are safe for long-term use with Greyhounds are available.

Not that long ago, the only answer to arthritis pain for dogs was either aspirin, which can upset the stomach, or cortisone, which can cause an array of side effects when used long term. This new class of drug can put the zip back into your dog's step and increase his interest in walking and even running. Ask your veterinarian if it would be appropriate for your dog.

CHECK BLOOD VALUES

Many medical conditions, such as decreased kidney or liver function, can be detected by having your veterinarian perform a complete blood scan. This should be done yearly on any dog over the age of seven. If a problem is detected early, you may be able to head off trouble with medication or even a change in diet.

SAYING GOOD-BYE

I won't deny that the end of a dog's life is a wrenching experience for an owner. As the head of an adoption agency, I not only have to deal with the passing of my own dogs but also hear of the passing of dogs that I have adopted out. While it is all very sad, it also has been very meaningful to me. I am constantly moved by how many people feel profoundly changed by their dogs.

Whether you have had your dog for two years or twelve, the final good-bye is just as hard. I do not believe that people should ever be told that their dog would be better off euthanized. The decision to euthanize is a very personal one. Most people who suggest euthanasia are just trying to be helpful and to remind you that there is a way to end your dog's suffering — but the final choice is yours alone.

When my dear King was diagnosed with cancer at the age of 13½, one of my concerns was, How will I know when it is time to let him go? My veterinarian told me, "Don't worry, you'll know." I couldn't imagine how that would be true. And yet, two months later, one day I looked at King, he looked back, and I knew. It

The old guard, Jasper (foreground) and King.

didn't make it any less sad, but at least I had the strong feeling that his life at that point involved more pain than pleasure and that he was ready to go. I was with King as the vet administered the final needle, and as he went into the next world, I told him how much I loved him. That is all we can do for our dogs, but it is no small thing.

Old age for a dog does not have to mean misery either for you or for him. When you reflect on all the pleasure dogs bring you during the course of their life, I'm sure you'll agree that they are worth making a few modifications for so that they can maintain their dignity and you can continue to be enriched by their company.

Chapter Six

Insecticides and Anesthesia

*A*s you've probably already realized, Greyhounds are very sensitive creatures. What you may not know, however, is that this sensitivity also extends to their reactions to certain drugs and chemicals. The information in this chapter will help you provide safe relief for your dog from such pests as fleas, as well as enable you to discuss with your veterinarian the anesthesia best suited for Greyhounds should the need arise.

FLEA COLLARS

In our attempt to rid our pets from fleas, we Americans have exposed ourselves, and our animals, to an assortment of toxic chemicals. Take, for example, seemingly innocuous flea collars. They are sold everywhere, and one could almost be lulled into thinking that they are both safe and effective. In fact, they are neither. Standard flea collars have their origins in nerve-gas chemical warfare, and they work by permeating the skin of your animal's neck and, eventually, paralyzing and killing the flea that bites the skin. They should never encircle the neck of a Greyhound nor, in my opinion, any other animal.

Some of the chemicals commonly found in flea collars can, in a Greyhound and other sensitive and/or allergic animals, cause nausea, convulsions and even death.

An added hazard is that we dispose of over 50 million of these collars every year, which means that they add to the already growing toxic-waste problem we face in this country.

In general, I believe we, as a culture, have become far too casual in our use of toxic chemicals. One look at the state of our air and water will confirm that. So, too, have we become too casual about the chemicals we put on our pets. As it turns out, because of the way their bodies metabolize these substances, Greyhounds are extremely sensitive to many pesticides, so there is no margin for error.

Similarly, the chemical compounds found in various flea shampoos, dips and sprays can be equally deadly.

INSECTICIDES

Most insecticides can be grouped into one of three families: the organophosphates, the carbamates and the pyrethrins. Neither the first nor the second should ever be considered for use on Greyhounds.

ORGANOPHOSPHATES

Some examples of organophosphates are malathion, Diazinon and chlorpyrifos (sold as Dursban®), all of which are used in various potent flea killers. As with flea collars, I don't believe any animal (or human) should be exposed to them, but especially not Greyhounds. A recent study conducted at the University of Washington showed that even a single episode of poisoning worthy of treatment could lead to "a persistent decline in neuropsychological performance."

CARBAMATES

The next group, carbamates, includes carbaryl (sold as Sevin®) as well as other carbamate compounds. These, too, hold the potential for a bad reaction, either in the short term with immediate symptoms (such as profuse salivating, labored breathing, vomiting and so on) or in the long term (nervous system damage or cancer).

Pyrethrins

Pyrethrins are the least toxic of the three and are a natural substance derived from the chrysanthemum flower. Pyrethroids (such as permethrin, allethrin and resmethrin) are man-made equivalents. They are strong enough to kill most fleas but have a very low toxicity level for mammals. It is very popular to mix pyrethrins with piperonyl butoxide. This is a synergist that, although toxic, can be used sparingly (combined with pyrethrins) if an infestation is especially severe.

Also to be avoided are chemicals (cythioate, propoxur and fenthion) that are applied monthly to the length of the dog's spine or in a spot on the base of the neck (sold as Rabon®, Baygon®, ProSpot®, Ex-Spot® and others). They are much too strong for a Greyhound, and you are risking damage or, possibly, death. In general, if a product says "safe for puppies and kittens" it will be safe for a Greyhound.

NEW PRODUCTS

In the last few years several new products to combat fleas and ticks have appeared on the market. The following are safe for Greyhounds, and I would go so far as to say that now there is no need for a dog to ever suffer from these pests again.

Lufenuron

Lufenuron (marketed under the name Program®) is a once-a-month flea reproduction inhibitor. It is not an insecticide and will not kill fleas. However, the eggs produced by fleas that have fed on a treated dog will not hatch. Eventually, if all the pets in a home are treated, home infestation can be prevented. The drawbacks are that it takes a while to work, you must treat all of the animals in a household and the fleas must bite a treated animal for the flea to become sterile. If an animal has a flea allergy (flea dermatitis) it will aggravate the condition. Program should be used in combination with insecticides to improve its effectiveness. The cost of treatment is about $6.50 a month.

IMIDACLOPRID

Imidacloprid (marketed under the name Advantage®) is a topical insecticide that kills fleas on contact, before they can lay eggs, so it breaks the flea life cycle. A few drops are applied once a month directly on the dog's (or cat's) skin. It spreads on the skin's surface and remains effective even after bathing or swimming. The advantage (no pun intended) is that it actually kills the fleas, it works within 24 hours and the animal does not have to by bitten by fleas for it to work. The disadvantages are that it is only available from veterinarians and it is rather expensive, about $10.00 a month. Compared to constant flea dipping, exterminators and relentless house cleaning, though, it seems well worth the price.

FIPRONIL

Fipronil (marketed under the name Frontline®) is a topical insecticide that kills both fleas and ticks. One application kills fleas on dogs for up to three months and ticks for up to a month. Like Advantage it works within 24 to 48 hours and is not significantly affected by shampooing or swimming. Its chief advantages are that it kills both fleas and ticks and the cost is reasonable, about $11.00, for an ampule that will kill fleas for three months and ticks for one.

SELAMECTIN

Selamectin (marketed under the name Revolution®) is a monthly topical insecticide that not only prevents and controls fleas and their eggs, but is also effective against ear mites, sarcoptic mites and American dog ticks, and even prevents heartworm disease. It works within 36 hours of application, has been tested safe for Greyhounds, and makes it easy to prevent fleas and heartworm with just one product. The downside is that it is rather expensive (about $25 per application) and does not kill deer ticks, which carry Lyme disease.

AMITRAZ

Amitraz is the active ingredient in tick collars marketed under the names of Preventic® and Tick Arrest®. This collar is not to be confused with standard, toxic flea collars. Amitraz is carried in the oils of the dog's skin, paralyzes the mouth of the tick and detaches 99 percent of ticks within 24 hours. The collar is good for about 75 days, but it is a good idea to remove it before shampooing or letting your dog swim, as these may reduce its effectiveness.

Although the collar is nontoxic to Greyhounds if worn, it is very toxic if they somehow chew on a collar. Make sure the collar is tight enough that it makes contact with the skin. Clip off any excess material once the collar is fastened. If you have more than one dog and they play-bite each other's neck, this is not the product for you. The cost of a collar ranges from $10.00 to $18.00, depending on whether you buy from a veterinarian or a retailer. Do not use a collar containing Amitraz if your dog (of any breed) is taking any of the following medications: Clomicalm, Elavil, Clomipramine, Anipryl or Phenylpropanolamine.

Although these new products have been tested safe for Greyhounds, it is possible that your dog may have an allergic reaction. This is true of all drugs and even foods, and does not mean that the products are not safe for Greyhounds in general. It just means that you may have an allergic dog.

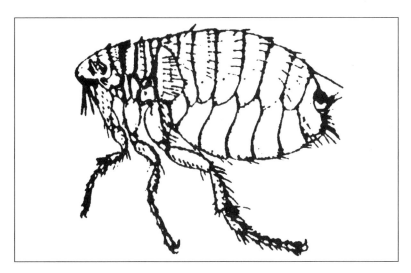

One of the 2,237 species of fleas.

NATURAL FLEA CONTROL

I know how maddening an infestation of fleas can be, and so here are some effective, nontoxic ways to deal with the problem.

First of all, it is important to treat your home and not just the dog. Fleas come from the environment, so you must eliminate them there. Vacuum daily and throw away the vacuum bag. Wash the dog's bedding frequently. Heat also kills fleas, so you can toss the dog's pillows in a hot dryer.

INSECT GROWTH REGULATOR

A relatively new product, which is called an insect growth regulator (IGR), eliminates fleas by preventing them from reproducing. Given that two adult fleas can produce over one million offspring in a year, it is essential that their reproductive cycle be broken. Generally, the products, which go by the trade names of Precor® and Torus®, are sprayed all over the house and in the animal's sleeping areas. One warning: Sometimes companies combine IGR's with toxic chemicals. Make sure what you buy (or what you have applied by an exterminator) is in its pure form.

HERBAL PREPARATIONS

The only completely safe products to apply directly to your Greyhound's skin are herbal formulas, which vary in effectiveness, and pyrethrins. Most herbs simply drive fleas away but don't kill them. Pyrethrins work by literally choking fleas to death. Pyrethrin formulas are found in powders and shampoos, but read the label carefully and avoid toxic additives.

DIETARY ADDITIVES

Some people use dietary means to control fleas. One woman I know dusts her dogs with brewer's yeast weekly and adds it to the animals' food. Many people report success with garlic capsules. Still others swear by the addition of vitamins. I have tried all of the above with little success. They do serve, however, to bolster your dog's immune system, so, if for no other reason, they may be worth a try.

THE FLEA COMB

There is one surefire, totally nontoxic way to keep fleas (and ticks) from your Greyhound. It's by using a flea comb, and while it is anything but a high-tech device, it really works! I comb my dogs (and cats) daily and find that although it is a bit time-consuming, it is a way to groom your animal safely and spend some time with him.

The best way to use a flea comb is to first get set up with two bowls of water: one soapy and warm, the other clear and warm. Then place your pet right next to the soapy water bowl. Now comb through once (with the hair, not against it), and you'll see fleas (if there are any) and flea dirt trapped between the fine teeth of the comb. Immediately dip the comb in the soapy water. The dirt will fall off, and the fleas will drown as the soap clogs their lungs. Make sure the comb is flea free, then rinse in clear water before you make the next pass through the animal's fur. You'll see that the dog will come to enjoy the combing both for the relief it brings and for the time you're spending with him.

HOW TO REMOVE A TICK

Ticks are hard to remove because their mouth parts are barbed and they also secrete a sticky substance that holds the mouth in place while feeding. If you remove a tick incorrectly you will cause it to release the very toxins you are trying to avoid.

Do not use your fingers. Use tweezers or a specially made tick-removal device. Grasp the tick's body and pull away from the point of attachment. Do not jerk or twist. If the mouth breaks off, use a sterilized needle to remove it as you would a splinter.

Wash the bite area with soap and water, and apply an antiseptic, such as alcohol. Wash your hands thoroughly with soap and very warm water. Mark the date of the tick bite on the calendar and watch for symptoms of disease in upcoming weeks.

PARASITE CONTROL

Ridding your Greyhounds of internal parasites has been made considerably easier by a product that was introduced a few years ago. The drug combination of praziquantel/pyrantel pamoate/febantel (marketed under the name Drontal Plus®) is the best choice, because it is the only product that kills hookworms, roundworms, whipworms *and* tapeworms. In addition, unless a dog is severely infested, one dose of the tablets, given with a little food, may be all your dog needs.

Intestinal worms, however, are not the only thing that can lodge in the intestines. Another condition your Greyhound may have (especially if he is experiencing frequent bouts of diarrhea or loose stools) is giardiasis (caused by a microscopic parasite called *Giardia lambli*). If symptoms are present and your dog has already been dewormed, ask your vet to run a test for giardiasis. Should it come back positive, metronidazole is the drug treatment of choice.

Task® is definitely not recommended for use against worms in Greyhounds, as it has an organophosphate base. As you now know, Greyhounds are extremely sensitive to this substance, and you could very well create more problems than you would solve. Be sure to make your veterinarian aware of this if he is not already.

Some people routinely deworm their dogs, which constitutes a severe misuse of a toxic substance. Even some veterinarians have been known to dispense dewormers without having performed a fecal test. Dogs should only be dewormed if a fecal sample has been microscopically examined by a veterinarian and found to contain parasites. Dewormers are toxic and can build up in a dog's system over time and irritate his intestines. Furthermore, overuse of dewormers will bring about resistant strains of parasites, much the way antibiotics are overused and have given way to resistant strains of bacteria. The old adage "Kill the worm, not the dog" should be kept in mind. If your yard has parasites which continually reinfect your dog, treat your yard, and keep the dog out of it until the problem is resolved.

This 15th-century French print shows
Greyhounds being treated by "veterinarians."

ANESTHESIA AND THE GREYHOUND

How they respond to anesthesia is another way in which Greyhounds (and other sighthounds) are different from other breeds of dogs. If you think your veterinarian may not be familiar with these differences, you might want to lend him or her this book so he can read the next section for up-to-date information on the subject.

One reason Greyhounds react as they do to drugs is that their liver metabolizes them more slowly. Another factor is the breed's low percentage of body fat proportionate to its size. Greyhounds have, on the average, 16 percent body weight of fat as compared with 35 percent in mixed-breed dogs of similar weight. The level of some drugs in a dog's system falls by going into its fat. The less fat, the longer it takes for the blood level to fall.

Certain forms of anesthesia are safer than others for Greyhounds. Bear in mind that all anesthesia, whether for dogs or humans, carries some risk. Never avoid necessary surgery because of this risk, but do select a veterinarian who will talk with you and choose the safest type of anesthesia and administer it in the safest way. (Also, when practical, combine procedures such as spaying or neutering with a teeth cleaning. That way a dog only has to be anesthetized once.)

Dr. Alan Klide, associate professor of veterinary anesthesia at the University of Pennsylvania School of Veterinary Medicine, has this to say about anesthesia for Greyhounds: "It is common practice to give a drug to calm dogs before anesthesia is begun and also to give them one to make them dry and prevent the heart from slowing. If Greyhounds are given a higher dose of narcotic, then they will need less thiobarbiturate. There are many narcotics, but the one that is most useful and safe, in dogs, is called oxymorphone. Glycopyrrolate, one of two drugs used to dry secretions, allows the dogs to wake up sooner than if the other drug, atropine, is used."

THIOBARBITURATES

Further, Dr. Klide suggests:

"This whole problem can be avoided by not using a thiobarbiturate. There are other drugs that can be injected to begin anesthesia. One called methohexital is commonly used by veterinarians to anesthetize Greyhounds. There are two relatively new intravenous anesthetics which look promising for anesthetizing Greyhounds, and these are propofol and ctomidate.

"There are several inhaled anesthetics which are used in veterinary and human anesthesia. In general, halothane is well tolerated in normal individuals. A newer anesthetic which may be useful in some circumstances is isoflurane."

My own experience with sighthounds and anesthesia is that recovery seems quickest when isoflurane is used. But not all delays in recovery can be traced to the type of anesthesia used. In some cases when it takes a dog an excessive amount of time to regain consciousness, there is often an underlying problem that delays recovery. Complete blood tests, especially on dogs over the age of five, should be run before a dog is given anesthesia because many health problems can be detected in advance.

MALIGNANT HYPERTHERMIA

Greyhounds can experience a further reaction to anesthesia. Dr. Klide explains:

"There is a disease of humans and some animals which is rare, but very severe. It has been reported in Greyhounds. It is called malignant hyperthermia. When the individual with this condition is stressed or anesthetized with certain anesthetics, including all the available inhaled ones, they get very hot, may get stiff and will probably die unless they are given a drug called dantrolene. If a dog or its relatives has such a condition in its history, it should be given dantrolene before, during and for a few days after it is anesthetized.

"When other drugs such as sedatives or tranquilizers need to be given to Greyhounds, if possible, a low dose should be tried first."

WAYS TO SPEED RECOVERY

To discourage a prolonged recovery in a Greyhound, Dr. Klide notes the following:

- "Intravenous fluids may have to be limited because of heart disease.
- Keep the dog warm; cold prolongs the depth and duration of anesthesia.
- Provide mechanical ventilation if necessary.
- Administer oxygen if necessary.
- Turn the dog periodically to try to prevent the occurrence of pneumonia.
- Measure blood sugar and make normal if not normal."

For exact drugs and dosages, please see Appendix Three. You may want to copy the section and give it to your veterinarian before your dog has any surgery.

Are your dogs safe from the hazards of herbicides?

LAWN CHEMICALS AND CANINE CANCER

One final piece of advice pertains to the use of herbicides on your lawn. There was a time when people (and companies) would use whatever chemicals were needed to rid a lawn of weeds and promote green grass. Not so anymore.

A commonly used weed-killing chemical compound called 2, 4-D has been linked to cancer in dogs. In fact, dogs that walk on treated lawns are twice as likely to develop lymphatic cancer. And, if the lawn is treated four or more times a year, a dog's risk of developing cancer doubles. Studies are now underway to see what health hazards are posed to humans. So, if you value your dog's health (and possibly your own), avoid the use of herbicides on your lawn.

If your dog is accidentally exposed to herbicides, wash his paws immediately with soap and water, make sure he doesn't lick his paws and keep an eye on him. If he exhibits any signs of poisoning such as salivating, disorientation or vomiting, take him to a veterinarian immediately.

Chapter Seven

Training

*W*hen you adopt a retired racing Greyhound, you are getting a dog that is already extensively trained. Since you are getting an adult dog and most of the training has already been done for you, don't think that any complicated or extensive training measures are needed. They're not! There are, however, some things your Greyhound has learned that are irrelevant to his new life as a companion. As such, there are some new tricks you must teach this "old" dog as well as some old tricks you must help him forget.

It is uncanny how most Greyhounds seem to be right at home even though they've never before been in a house. I've concocted a rather elaborate legend to explain this.

Long ago, in a racing kennel far away, a Greyhound went home for the night with his trainer. He was a very intelligent and very observant Greyhound, because when he went back to the kennel the next day he was able to recount to his fellow racers every detail of what it was like to spend the night in a house. Because he was a Greyhound that was exceptionally fond of pleasure, he gave special attention to details of soft places to sleep and where the food was kept.

Since the other Greyhounds had little to occupy their minds with other than thoughts of chasing the lure, they took great delight in these tales of home life. And so, by oral tradition, the story spread. Mother Greyhounds told the tale to their young pups. Old male Greyhounds told it to young males. Over the years the details of what it was like to live in a house spread to

*Ajax carries his pillow everywhere and
uses it for — what else? — a head rest!*

every racing kennel in the land. And that is why Greyhounds behave as if they've waited all their lives for the experience of living with you — because they have!

Unfortunately, over the years some of the story became exaggerated (that Greyhounds are to be fed steak upon request), while other parts were left out entirely (like the fact that not everyone wants a dog on the sofa). So now it is up to you to set the record straight and establish the rules of the house.

HOUSEBREAKING

One rule that everyone will agree on is that the dog must be housebroken. The reason for it is obvious. What is not so obvious to some people is how to accomplish it.

You have a leg up (no pun intended) on the process by virtue of the fact that racing dogs have already been crate-trained. In the kennels, Greyhounds are housed in large crates (cages) and are let out four times a day to exercise and relieve themselves. For most dogs it does not take a very big leap of the imagination to see your entire house as a crate.

The first thing you need to do is keep your dog on a schedule. As much as possible, try to adapt yours to his. In other words, if you usually get up at nine in the morning but you know the dog is used to waking at seven, get up earlier at first, then gradually change the dog's sleeping patterns.

TAKE THE DOG OUT OFTEN

The basics of housebreaking apply to racing Greyhounds just like any other breed. Walk the dog first thing in the morning, after both meals, midday if possible, and before bed. Keep an eye on the dog in between, too. If he seems restless and begins pacing, he may need to go out. Bear in mind that the dog may be a little uneasy in his new surroundings, and this, combined with new food and water and a new schedule, may affect his bowels and bladder.

USE THE CRATE

In Chapter Four I talked about the importance of crates in easing the transition from kennel to home. Most of what was said there concerned preventing the dog from hurting himself or becoming destructive in the home. Yet crates are useful tools for housebreaking, too.

Since racing Greyhounds are crate-trained, you can prevent "accidents" in the house by putting the dog in a crate. They have been trained not to soil their crates, and rare indeed is the Greyhound that will.

If you take your dog out four or five times a day, if you keep an eye on him the rest of the time and if the dog sleeps in the crate at night, there is little room for error.

There are exceptions, of course.

I have found that a few modest Greyhounds are uncomfortable relieving themselves while someone is holding them on a leash. You can walk them for miles, but if they know you're there watching, they won't do their "business." Later, this type of dog, in desperation, usually finds a remote corner of the house in which to relieve himself. What should you do? The answer is simple: If you have a fenced yard, let him run loose. But what if you don't? You have three choices: find a fenced area, fence in a small area yourself or require the dog to get used to being on-lead. The second or third choices are the ones you will eventually make, because it certainly isn't very convenient to travel to someone else's fenced yard four times a day just so your dog can have some privacy!

If you decide just to tough it out and make your dog comply, then you might consider using an extendable leash so that the dog can get at least 10 or 20 feet away from you. One word of caution, though: Extendable leashes come in a plastic box with a handle. The leash extends from there, much like a tape measure. The design flaw is that it is very easy for it to be pulled out of your hand if the dog gives a sudden lunge. Then not only will your dog be running loose but the noise of the plastic box scraping along the sidewalk may scare your Greyhound into running even more. If you choose to use an extendable leash, make sure you also buy a safety wrist loop that attaches to the plastic handle on one end and over your wrist on the other. The loops are very inexpensive and could save your dog's life.

Extendable leashes are only safe when used with a wrist loop.

BEHAVIORAL "ACCIDENTS"

Some "accidents" are not accidents at all. Generally speaking, they have their root in one of three causes: health problems, territorial marking or unhappiness. I do not believe that dogs eliminate in the house out of spite.

HEALTH PROBLEMS

Before you begin any behavior modification, eliminate the possibility of a health problem. Diarrhea or persistent urinating in the house may be signs that something is physically wrong. Parasites and urinary tract infections are common causes of housebreaking problems. Have your dog checked by a veterinarian, especially if he was housebroken then suddenly isn't.

TERRITORIAL MARKING

For some dominant dogs the urge to stake her (or his) claim is just too strong for her own good. To correct her, you need to catch her in the act, tell her "No!" firmly but gently, and then escort her outside. When she does relieve herself outside, praise her profusely (positive reinforcement). If you cannot keep an eye on a dog who you know has a tendency to mark, crate her until you are sure she knows the rules of the house.

You must be consistent and react the same way every time. Don't scream, Greyhounds are far too sensitive for that. And of course, never, ever strike them. A serious tone of voice, coupled with regular use of the crate, is all you will need.

AN UNHAPPY CAMPER

Of course, it is impossible to know exactly why a particular dog is unhappy. It could be that they are lonely, bored or anxious. But whatever the reason, some dogs either urinate or defecate in response to unhappiness. If you have ruled out health problems, are sure you are taking the dog out often enough, have rigorously addressed the marking issue and can do no more to change the dog's environment (for example, cannot fence your yard, cannot get another dog, cannot spend more time at home, etc.), then you must consider the possibility that yours is just not the right home for the dog. It doesn't mean you have a bad home — just that it might not be the right fit for the dog.

There have been times when a dog has been returned to me because the people said they just could not housebreak her. As if by magic, once the dog was transferred to an experienced foster home, she was completely housebroken and never had even one accident. When that happens, we know the dog just wasn't happy where she was. Maybe she needed a fenced yard and didn't have one. Maybe he needed the company of another dog and was simply lonely. Maybe she was in a noisy house and wanted peace and quiet. Maybe he didn't like being left alone for eight hours every day. If you have done everything else according to the book (visited the veterinarian, used a crate, praised good behavior and have done your best to alter what you could), and you are still having a problem, it might be time to talk to your adoption group to see if they think an exchange is in order.

OBEDIENCE TRAINING

I recommend a basic obedience course to everyone who adopts an ex-racer. A well-trained dog is a real asset. Not only is he easier to live with, but also he has a very clear idea of his boundaries and becomes comfortable and secure knowing that when he does what you want, you are happy with him. Most dogs, and especially Greyhounds, are eager to please.

A dog's training could also save his life. A dog that is out of control rarely remains with the same family who originally adopted him. Take a visit to any animal shelter and you will see many dogs, purebreds and mixed breeds alike, that never had the benefit of basic training. Sadly, most of them will be euthanized because when people are looking to adopt a dog, the trained ones are the first to be chosen. Should your dog ever have to be readopted, good training is an investment in his future. How many people do you know who would be interested in adopting an older dog that chews shoes, jumps up on people and pulls on the leash?

Choosing a Good Trainer

There is no special requirement for a basic obedience course other than that it be accomplished humanely. The best trainers are the ones who teach a dog by praise rather than fear. This technique is known as positive reinforcement. Greyhounds are extremely sensitive, and if the course instructor believes in shouting, instilling fear, using choke collars with metal prongs or, worst of all, electric shocks, don't walk away, run! I have seen Greyhounds that have endured cruel training, and they have never recovered. Their spirit was broken, and they developed many neurotic habits as a result.

You should also decline to participate in a program if the teachers recommend leaving the dog behind so they can train him alone. A wonderful bond is established between you and your dog when you take an obedience course together. Actually, you are both being trained — you are being trained as the pack leader, and the dog is being trained to look to you for guidance. By leaving the job to someone else, there will always be a missing link. Besides, who knows what kind of training will take place after you've gone home?

The best trainers are the ones who teach a dog by praise rather than fear. Additionally, a trainer should be aware of the temperament differences between breeds and train accordingly. Greyhounds, for example, do not respond to commands the same way German Shepherds do. All lessons should be tailored to the breed.

Getting the Greyhound to Sit

Frequently I am asked, "Can Greyhounds sit?" My answer is "Yes, but most of them prefer not to." It isn't painful for them, but I get the distinct impression that it is uncomfortable. Usually you'll find a Greyhound in one of three poses: standing, crouching (with forelegs extended, chest resting on the floor) or lying on his side. There's nothing wrong with any of these postures except that they take up a bit of room. If you insist that the dog be taught to sit, train him the same way you'd train any other dog. Gently pull up on his collar while pushing down on his rump. He

Oscar shows off his AKC Canine Good Citizen award,
proving that Greyhounds certainly can sit!

may not get it at first, but with practice he will. By the way, one myth that has been circulating is that racing Greyhounds are trained not to sit so they will leave the starting box quicker. This is not true. Racing dogs are naturally eager to take off, and sitting is the last thing on their minds.

TOOLS OF THE TRADE

THE MUZZLE

All racing dogs are transported with muzzles. In the Introduction, I explained that it is not because Greyhounds are vicious, but rather, because all dogs are more prone to aggression when they are under stress, be it the stress of chasing a lure or of traveling in close quarters.

When you adopt an ex-racer, the muzzle should be part of his "dowry." It will become an essential part of training him when he first meets your other pets.

Most Greyhounds are excellent with small dogs and cats. A few aren't. You don't want to find out which category he falls into the hard way. Exercise caution. Just because the dog is wonderful and affectionate with you, that doesn't mean he wouldn't chase, and kill, a cat. And the fact that he gets along with dogs his own size doesn't mean he would be able to resist catching your toy dog.

Even if you don't have other pets, a muzzle can come in handy in the future. If he is not good about having his nails trimmed, a muzzle is invaluable. Additionally, if he will be running with other dogs in a fenced area, they all should be muzzled.

Racing muzzles, made of molded plastic, are used only during a race.

THE CORRECT COLLAR

When walking your dog on a leash, always use a choke collar. The reason for this is simple: the head of a Greyhound is very narrow, and a regular collar would have to be kept on so tightly that it would choke the dog continually. At the racetrack, leashes are rarely used; the person leading the dog uses the dog's collar as a handle. That way the dog cannot escape. But in life on the outside it is not practical to hold your dog by the collar.

A choke collar will stay slack until the moment it is needed, and only then will it tighten up. You would be amazed at the ease with which a regular collar can slip right over a Greyhound's ears. Before you know it, the dog is gone and you are left holding an empty collar. Some Greyhounds are quite expert at backing out of their collars, too. Regular collars are fine for wear around the house and to hold ID and rabies tags, but some sort of a restraining collar is essential for use on the street. Many people I know keep a choker and leash permanently attached and slip them on the dog as they go out and slip them off when they come in. The people who do this keep a regular collar (with ID tags) on at all times, just in case the dog ever dashes out the door. The choker is used only for walks. There is always the possibility, albeit remote, that a choke collar could get caught on something and actually choke the dog when you aren't around, so it's best to reserve its use for the leash only.

"HUMANE" CHOKE COLLARS

Of the various choke collars on the market, the one I recommend, and indeed the one I give out with each adoption, has a slightly different construction from the traditional choker. It consists of two flat nylon circles, a smaller one intertwined with the larger. When the choke action is needed, it restrains the dog firmly and securely yet never pinches the throat or gags the dog. This type of collar is known generically as either a martingale collar or as a humane choker. As far as I'm concerned, no Greyhound should be without one.

The collar no Greyhound should be without.
Tracey models the humane choker.

If you choose to use a standard choke collar, make it a flat or rounded nylon one rather than a chain choker. Greyhound skin is too sensitive for the metal ones.

HOLDING THE LEASH PROPERLY

While we are on the subject of collars, let me say a few words about leashes. Many people do not hold a leash correctly. There is a reason that there is a loop at one end of the leash, and that is so you can put your hand through it. Only once the loop is over your hand and is resting around the outside of your wrist do you take hold of the leash. Holding the leash correctly prevents it from ever slipping out of your hand.

We have come to call the correct way of holding the leash the "Greyhound Grip," and everyone who adopts from us, whether or not they have ever before owned a dog, gets a 10-second demonstration on the right way to hold the leash. Those of us involved in adopting out these dogs are acutely aware of how important it is to hold tight.

Do Wacka Do, 1989 Iowa Distance Champion,
shows off a slip-lead for quick release in lure coursing.

As for what type of leash to get, I recommend either four- or six-foot lengths. If your dog is a chewer, try a metal chain leash. Otherwise, nylon or leather will do nicely. There is no particular advantage to the extendable/retractable leash, but the disadvantages are that the dog can get farther away from you and can easily get tangled up around you or something else and the leash, in general, provides less control. And, as I said earlier, they should never be used without the safety wrist loop accessory.

USING A HARNESS

If you choose to use a harness rather than a collar and leash, fine. A harness does provide good control, but it is somewhat of a nuisance to put on and take off. It should, of course, be taken off when not needed, as it can chafe and irritate a dog's skin. Don't forget to keep the appropriate ID tags, licenses and so on attached to a collar. You never want your dog to be without identification, even at home.

Just because you choose to use a harness doesn't mean you can tie the dog in the yard either on a runner or to a stake. With a dog capable of reaching high speeds in a short period of time, even the snapping back of a harness when the dog reaches the end of his tether could injure him severely.

Most Greyhounds do not pull while on-lead. For the few that do, the best method of control is a no-pull halter. It gives the dog a humane tug under the arms when he pulls too hard and reminds him to stay in line.

Remember, walk a Greyhound on a leash or release him in a completely fenced area only.

This is a chapter that you may want to read over a few times. The information in it comes from personal experiences I have had with these wonderful dogs. If you can learn from some of the mistakes that others have made, then perhaps those mistakes were not in vain. And, once you and your dog have reached an understanding with each other about the way things are, you will have the best companion in the world.

MEETING OTHER DOGS

To introduce your new Greyhound to his new housemates that are dogs his own size (or any size down to about 20 pounds), let them first sniff each other with a closed door between them. Dogs can tell a lot about each other from their scent. Let them have plenty of time to get the full doggy bouquet; then, with both the Greyhound and your other dog on leashes, let them meet. The best place for their first meeting is on neutral territory and, preferably, outside. A lot more sniffing will occur. If you see either dog's hackles rise, move them apart. It is only one Greyhound in a million that will start a fight with another dog, so if either is the instigator, it will probably be your other dog. Gradually they will establish which one is dominant, and they will probably become best friends.

MEETING VERY SMALL DOGS AND CATS

If you have small dogs or cats, bring your Greyhound into the house on a leash and *wearing his muzzle.* This is essential because, as you know by now, Greyhounds are terribly fast. Should they pull the leash away from you, at least you'll have the insurance of a muzzle. I once heard of a couple who adopted out Greyhounds advising new owners not to use the muzzle on the theory that they would be giving the dog a mixed message. They incorrectly thought that by using the muzzle you would be indicating to the dog that it was time to race. Nothing could be further from the truth. The racing muzzles are of a completely different construction from the type you will get, which are used only when the dogs travel or are turned out together. Believe me, the racers know the difference!

I remember that when I adopted my original Greyhound, King, I told the person from whom I took him that if he went after my cats I would have to return him. As it turned out, he was terrified of the cats and trembled and cried during the first month he was with them. Needless to say, we had no trouble. My second Greyhound, Ajax, was totally unafraid and barely acknowledged the cats' existence. No trouble there, either.

Signs of trouble are when the dog actively lunges at the small pets, barks or growls or is just too interested. A certain degree of interest is normal. They are sighthounds, after all, and they respond to visual stimuli. But "too much interest" is when they literally can't take their eyes off the pet, they begin to crouch down as if to spring forward or they whine in the direction of where they last saw the pet. Should you see any of these signs, keep the muzzle on and keep the dog on a leash, and under no circumstances should you leave them alone together.

To correct a dog that may see these small pets as prey, use a choke collar, and whenever he attempts to lunge, jerk the collar and firmly say "No." Eventually you will "deprogram" any but the most intractable dog from his racing training. If a dog does not respond to your corrections within a few days, think about exchanging him for a dog that does not have the chasing urge so deeply ingrained. For some dogs, no amount of correcting will work, and you don't want a tragedy on your hands. By the way, even though most dogs eventually will respect the small pets in the house, outside may be a different story. The house, after all, is your domain, but as far as they are concerned, outside is up for grabs. You'll have to teach them otherwise, the same way you taught them inside.

Boof Man is so good with small animals that he even protects small kittens.

Don't be alarmed by the information you've just read in this section. Most Greyhounds are just fine with small pets. And even the ones that aren't initially can usually be trained into complying. I say "usually," because I believe there are a very few for which the racing instinct is just too strong. There are extreme ways to get a dog to stop chasing, but I prefer taking the dog back and placing it in another home where there will be no temptation. I care for cats and small dogs too much to jeopardize their lives, and I respect the Greyhounds too much to put them through strenuous and unkind training.

RETRIEVING A LOST GREYHOUND

You may recall that in the first chapter I discussed the hazards of intentionally letting an ex-racer run off-lead. There is always the chance, though, that it will happen unintentionally. Of course we can't control everything, but it is prudent to be as careful as possible.

If you experience the misfortune of having a Greyhound run away from you or your yard, there is one way of getting him back that is sometimes more effective than simply calling him. It involves using a device intended for hunting that simulates the sound of an animal in distress. It is usually referred to as a squawker. A similar device is also used at the track when, at the finish line, one of the dogs starts heading in the wrong direction. The sound of the squawker gets his attention there, and it may do the same in your neighborhood. Squawkers are available at hunting supply stores as well as through mail-order catalogs.

There are other steps to take to find your Greyhound besides the squawker. Keep in mind that time is of the essence and many trails go cold after a few days.

The first thing to do is notify the police, the local animal shelter, the animal control officer and any nearby veterinarians (including your own). Stress to them that the dog is a retired racer capable of great speeds and that he is gentle and frightened. Give them your work and home phone numbers, plus the dog's ear tattoos, a physical description of him and any identification he is wearing (adoption group tag number, rabies tag number, dog license number and so on) Make sure you also notify the group from whom you adopted since they may well be the first to get a call from someone who has found him. They may also have volunteers in your area that will be willing to help search or distribute flyers.

Posting and distributing flyers is essential. If you can deliver them door to door, so much the better. Put them in supermarkets, store fronts, vet's offices, anywhere where people congregate.

Children are a great resource because they visit friends in neighborhoods and travel on school buses. They are also frequently in people's backyards, areas where you may not be able to see while searching. Use them as lookouts, and give them your numbers. You might also try contacting local schools to see if they'd be willing to make an announcement over their loudspeakers.

If you have an answering machine, mention your lost dog in your outgoing message and ask people to hold the dog if they've found him. Offering a reward is optional. My experience has been that there are many people in the world who sympathize with losing a dog. They will help you, money or not. The word reward on a flyer may, however, attract attention. Be prepared to pay up if you make an offer.

Since dogs at the track run in ovals, they often travel the same way when they are loose. If you are lucky enough to see which direction he was headed in as he left, track him in ovals or circles. While you are searching for him, it is often helpful to bring other Greyhounds, as the sight and scent of them may lure him to you.

Don't forget to place ads on the radio as well as in newspapers. Phrases like "owner heartsick" or "dog is frightened" strike a chord in other dog lovers and may improve your chances of eliciting help.

Finally, don't give up. We've had dogs on the loose for months that were eventually retrieved (although they caused us many sleepless nights). From time to time replace old signs and flyers with new ones that state that you're still looking. Make sure you list the date of disappearance, location, a complete description of the dog and several numbers where you can be reached. Again, ask people to hold the dog if they find him and stress that he is gentle but shy.

"INVISIBLE" FENCING

Frequently I am asked about fencing that is operated by a radio signal. If a dog crosses a predetermined boundary, a slight shock is delivered to his neck through a special collar. To put it simply, I don't like the system, and here's why.

I feel that racing Greyhounds have had quite enough negative reinforcement training to last them a lifetime. A shock to the neck, no matter how slight, would certainly be too much of a shock to the system for some of the more sensitive Greyhounds that I've met. Besides, I had a salesman of this type of system come to my property once, and I asked to feel the intensity of the shock collar. I put it against my leg (which I believe is less sensitive than a Greyhound's neck) and found it to be quite irritating. While not exactly painful, it was definitely startling and uncomfortable. I sent the man packing.

Another reason is that while these fences supposedly keep dogs in (and even that is up for debate — I once knew a Whippet named Wicket that would run through, shock or not) — they don't keep other dogs, animals or people out. So, a vicious neighborhood dog could come into your "protected" yard and attack your Greyhound. A rabid raccoon could do likewise. And, perhaps worst of all, a person could walk in and steal your Greyhound.

Housebreaking also can become a problem with invisible fencing. Dogs that were once perfectly trained can become so loathe to go outside because of the shock that they wind up doing their business in the house. I have known this to happen when several people did not follow my advice and installed these fences anyway. The dogs eventually were returned to us although we had a bit of a job rehabilitating them.

Finally, the speed with which Greyhounds run means that the length of time they are exposed to the correcting shock of the collar is very short — so short that it may not make a difference to them. Like little Wicket, they'll run through anyway.

HOME ALONE, YES — IN THE YARD ALONE, NO

Never leave your dog outside in the yard while you are not at home. Let me explain why.

A dog that may be perfectly calm in the yard as long as he knows you are in the house may go into a panic if he sees you drive away. Fear is a powerful emotion, and if the dog thinks he is somehow being abandoned, he is going to do everything possible to get to you. Everything may include jumping the fence, digging beneath it or even managing to unlatch the gate. Believe me, it has happened.

Another potential hazard in leaving a dog unattended in a fenced yard is that another animal may get in. A fight, started either by your dog, that is protecting his territory, or by the intruder, may ensue. Who will be there to break it up?

It's not only animals that can get into your yard. People can, too. It could be someone as innocuous as the meter reader, who doesn't latch the gate properly when he leaves, or it could be someone who steals dogs from unattended yards. There are such people who make their living by stealing dogs for resale to research laboratories.

Finally there is the weather to consider. Greyhounds have poor tolerance for both heat and cold. Think of the days when you leave for work and it is bright and sunny, then, out of nowhere, the clouds move in. Before you know it, the temperature has dropped 20 degrees and you wish you'd taken a sweater with you. Now think of the Greyhound with his thin skin and virtually no body fat. With neither fur nor fat for protection, Greyhounds are strictly indoor dogs.

By the way, while a dog door may be a convenience for you while you are home, make sure you bring your dogs in and lock the dog door before you leave. Many of the above cautions apply if you allow your dogs to go in and out while you're gone. To compound matters, other animals may even come into your house in pursuit of one of your hounds.

When the temperature dips below 32 degrees, Greyhounds need coats.

FENCING BASICS

Since the vast majority of Greyhounds are not jumpers, a fence four feet high will suffice, but never any lower. Remember, though, that the fence must be higher if it is erected on a hillside. The downward slope could give the dog an added height advantage. You will also be pleased to know that most are not diggers. In all of my adoptions, I've placed only four that were climbers, so for them, a chain link fence was out. Stockade or some sort of smooth wood was the only type that they could not climb.

SAFE, INEXPENSIVE FENCING

I am often asked what is the best type of fencing for ex-racers. Ideally, it should be smooth wood, six feet in height.

If money is a consideration, there is a safe, inexpensive fence you can install yourself with no tools other than a hammer. The fence is made of heavy green wire which comes in 50-foot rolls four feet high and is coated with a dark green vinyl. You need to buy metal stake-type fence posts that are five feet high and require no digging. You just hammer them into the ground (one foot underground, four feet above) at regular intervals, about every eight feet. If you place the stakes too far apart, the dogs can bend the wire down if they jump up on it. The wire is simply unrolled, stretched across your yard and attached to the little hooks protruding from the stakes.

Regardless of the type of fencing you have, always make sure the gates are closed. Don't assume that because they were closed yesterday they're still closed today. A heavy metal spring can be attached from the gate to the gate post so that it automatically slams shut. Also, check your fencing from time to time to be sure it's in good condition. I know from experience that things can happen, even to the best fencing. Always check your fencing after a bad storm. Not only might the fencing itself have been damaged, but fallen limbs from trees can pose a real hazard to your dog.

Finally, all fences should have a sign attached reminding people to latch the gate. Not only will it make them aware but also offers an added bonus: the fact that you keep large dogs may discourage intruders.

Chapter Eight

Having Fun

*T*he ways in which you can have fun with your ex-racer are limited only by your imagination. In fact, there are certain things you can do with Greyhounds that you can't do with any other breed of dog.

ARTIFICIAL LURE COURSING

Take, for example, artificial lure coursing. A plastic bag (or a rag or pelt) is dragged across a field by a motorized cord on a prede-termined course. It is virtually unknown outside sighthound cir-cles, and the reason is that the sport depends on the dog's ability to see the artificial lure and to take off after it. As we know, Greyhounds are sighthounds — they hunt by sight rather than by scent as do most other dogs. A Bloodhound would be dis-tinctly nonplussed at the sight of a white plastic bag being dragged across a field. In fact, when he could no longer see the bag, it would lose what little interest it held initially.

Not so with sighthounds. To them, a white plastic bag whip-ping across a field is enough to make them quiver in anticipation. It stirs up thousands of years of genetics (plus whatever training your racer had at the track) and is a sport made to order. Coursing as a sport grew out of the sighthounds' method of hunting. Not only do they hunt by sight, but they are also used to working as a team with others of their kind. Coursing makes use of both skills.

THE REQUIREMENTS

Specifically, the way a lure-coursing trial works is this:

All events held under the auspices of the American Sighthound Field Association (ASFA) or the American Kennel Club (AKC) allow the 11 sighthound breeds recognized by the AKC to compete: Afghan Hounds, Basenjis, Borzoi, Greyhounds, Ibizan Hounds, Irish Wolfhounds, Pharaoh Hounds, Rhodesian Ridgebacks, Salukis, Scottish Deerhounds and Whippets. The dogs must be at least a year old and registered with the American Kennel Club or the National Greyhound Association.

Since you have a former racer, the latter applies. In most circumstances you will not be able to get a copy of your Greyhound's NGA volume and certificate number. What you must do is apply to the AKC for an Indefinite Listing Privilege (ILP). This is not the same as an AKC breed registration, but it does allow a dog to compete in both ASFA- and AKC-sanctioned lure coursing events as well as AKC obedience trials, tracking tests and herding events. An ILP will only be issued to spayed or neutered dogs. Complete information is available from the AKC (address in Appendix Five).

Coursing events are held on an open field far from traffic and other hazards of civilization. All dogs must be kept on a leash or crated unless they are competing. On the day of the event, each hound that has been entered to participate must be present for roll call. At that time, all the hounds are checked for lameness and, in the case of bitches, to see if they are in heat. If either condition is present, the hound is excused, and the entry fee is returned. Dogs that have dewclaws, and almost all racers do, must have them taped to their legs so that they do not become tangled in the cord that pulls the lure.

Next, a random drawing takes place to determine the order in which the breeds compete. Only dogs of the same breed compete with each other (in other words, Greyhounds with Greyhounds, Borzois with Borzois and so on) and are run in groups of three (trios). If necessary, two dogs run together. After the preliminary course, during which each dog will have run twice and earned a certain number of points, another random draw is conducted to determine the order of breeds for the final courses. Dogs that have run together the first time around are not necessarily paired during the finals.

THE JUDGING

After the finals, the dogs with the highest scores compete with each other, and the winner of that course is designated Best of Breed. All dogs are ultimately working toward the title of Lure Courser of Merit, but that requires many points and many competitions. The main thing is to have fun and to watch your dog enjoy himself.

Lure coursing is an especially exciting sport because the dogs are judged by more than one criterion. A dog can get up to 100 points from each course, and the breakdown of maximum points per category is as follows:

Enthusiasm	15 points
Follow	15 points
Speed	25 points
Agility	25 points
Endurance	20 points

As you can see, this sport is not just about speed. Some of the dogs exhibit tremendous concentration (follow) and are distracted by nothing. Others excel in agility. This is seen when the lure is on a straight path and then abruptly takes a turn. An exceptionally agile dog can take a turn without missing a beat.

THE ACTION

At the start of the course, the hounds that have been selected to run together are each given a blanket of a different color. Their

Getting ready to slip the hounds.

collars are removed, and a quick-release collar (known as a slip-lead) is substituted. The trio is lined up at the starting line, and the owner or handler straddles the dog's back. The Huntmaster confirms that the dogs and the Lure Operator are ready. When the Huntmaster says the "T" sound of "Tally Ho!" the dogs are released (slipped).

The Lure Operator has an important job because it is up to him to make sure that the lure is just far enough ahead of the dogs so that they don't actually catch it, yet not so far that they lose interest. The Lure Operator must also be ready at a moment's notice to stop the lure should a dog accidentally get caught in the cord.

Most lure courses are between 500 and 1400 yards long. The cord is set out on an irregular course and is run through pulley stakes that are driven into the ground. There are several ways in which a dog can get injured during coursing, although all are relatively rare.

It is possible for a dog to get his foot caught in the cord. That could result in anything from a rope burn to a pulled tendon to a broken bone. Another hazard is that it is possible for dogs to

The chase.

Catching up with the lure — three white plastic bags.

collide. An extreme outcome of that could be a serious injury, but most likely a bumped dog will simply be thrown off course and lose time (and points).

CAUTIONS ABOUT COURSING

After getting you enthused about lure coursing, let me add some words of warning. Lure coursing is an extremely strenuous sport, and I believe the vast majority of ex-racers should not be involved with it or, if they are, not for too long. There are many reasons for this.

First of all, your Greyhound was retired for a reason. If he is five years of age or older, he was probably beginning to slow down after having had a winning career. Greyhounds are retired around that age because strenuous exercise is too hard on them at that point. This does not mean their lives are almost over, it just means that they are more suited to less taxing pursuits like long walks in the park.

If your Greyhound is younger than five, why was he retired? It is not always possible for the adoption agency to find out the exact cause of retirement; often they are just told the dog was not fast enough. But why wasn't he fast enough? Did he have an underlying medical condition that slowed him down or perhaps an undetected injury? Some injuries, such as a broken leg or dislocated toe, are obvious, but others do not show up until the dog is really active. By then it may be too late. If you are not absolutely certain why your Greyhound was retired, then a complete physical examination by your veterinarian, including blood tests and possibly X-rays, is in order.

Not all coursing fields are equal, either. Many sighthound breeds have a better innate ability to maneuver sharp corners than do Greyhounds. To compound it, our ex-racers were trained almost from birth to race in an oval pattern with no turns at all. Some courses are laid out with extremely sharp turns, which could seriously injure your dog if he doesn't do it right. Additionally, since most coursing fields are not fenced, they need to be well away from heavily traveled roads. Not all are. Don't believe it when people say that your Greyhound will be so transfixed by the lure that he'll never run away. I've seen it happen more than once.

I am sorry to say that I know of many people who have not exercised caution and who have coursed ex-racers with disastrous results. Some have coursed dogs that were overweight, some have coursed dogs that were too old and some have coursed dogs too often in a day. Some of the blame for this falls on a coursing club that will allow such practices. Unfortunately, inexperienced clubs and enthusiastic owners are a bad combination, and some dogs that were supposed to be enjoying their retirement years have been gravely injured.

Some clubs use the excuse that they are coursing just for fun, not for competition. What they fail to understand is that the dogs are completely unaware of whether or not their owner will get a ribbon or a trophy at the end of the session. All they know is that the lure is in motion and they're going after it. Greyhounds run even if it is not in their best interest. They will overcome pain to run, and they will ignore poor field conditions (hard ground, rutted or slippery surfaces and so on) or inclement weather (too hot, too cold or too humid). They depend on you, their guardian, to know right from wrong. I know that the sight of your hound chasing across a field is awe inspiring, but put your dog's welfare ahead of your entertainment. You owe him that much.

I have heard it said that a dog can injure himself even in his own backyard. This is true. But injuries are more likely on the coursing field. Also, no matter how fast your Greyhound tears around the backyard, it will neither be as fast nor with as much determination as when he is in pursuit of the lure.

To sum up, coursing is a wonderful sport best left to younger dogs, dogs that are exercised regularly (not just every other Sunday), and dogs that have been certified in good condition. The coursing club you participate with should be well experienced both in the operation of the lure and in first aid. Also, a veterinarian should be on call in case of a serious injury. People in charge of experienced clubs did not learn by trial and error. They learned from other experienced people and were smart enough to take their advice. The coursing field should have gentle, manageable turns for Greyhounds, and it should be far from traffic.

AMATEUR RACING

Amateur oval racing is another sport that is limited to sighthounds and it may be less taxing on former racers. These events, regulated by the National Oval Track Racing Association (NOTRA), run the dogs on an oval or u-val (U-shaped) track. Greyhounds and Whippets are considered the major breeds, while the other sighthounds are considered minor breeds.

Whippets and the minor breeds use the u-val track, while Greyhounds and Whippets use the oval track. The track surfaces are dirt or grass, and great care is taken to make sure they are very level. Continuous loop equipment pulls an artificial lure around the track, and dogs are judged on the order of the finish.

As a dog wins more heats (races) he accumulates more points, which lead to the Oval Racing Championship title (ORC). Points depend not only on where your dog finishes in a day's standing but also on how many other dogs competed that day as well as how many other dogs already have earned an ORC title.

Greyhounds and Whippets must use a starting box for oval racing. They must also be muzzled during the race and know how to use a starting box (no problem for an ex-racer). Because dogs can reach higher speeds on a track than on a lure course, even greater care must be taken to make sure that your dog is fit.

FUN RUNS

Another alternative to lure coursing adopted ex-racers is fun runs, sometimes organized by the adoption groups and other times just an informal gathering of enthusiastic owners. By getting ex-racers together in a large, fenced area such as a ball field, your dog can exercise and commune with others of his own breed while you can socialize with people with whom you have a lot in common — your love of these dogs.

To ensure the safety of your dog, I recommend strongly that the following safety tips be observed:

1. Have a vet examine your dog to make sure he is in good health and free of hidden injuries.

2. All dogs must be muzzled. If you have ever seen a dog fight you would understand this. Once aggression starts there is no stopping it, and all dogs, even the most mild mannered, will join in the fray.

3. Only ex-racers should be allowed to run — and not more than two dogs at a time. Even dogs that are "friends" while on-lead with their owner can become competitive while running free in a fenced area.

4. Make sure there are no small dogs or cats in the area. Even dogs that live with small creatures in the house may go after them outside. They don't need teeth to hurt them either. A sharp blow from a paw might be enough to break a small animal's back.

5. Do not allow your dog to run during the hottest time of the day or in very humid weather. Have fresh water available at all times, and make sure you walk the dog after he runs to help him cool down. Bring along a first-aid kit, too.

6. Always clean up after your dog.

A GREAT JOGGING COMPANION

Another activity that is a natural for Greyhounds is jogging — not alone, of course, but with you. While Greyhounds basically are sprinters, as opposed to long-distance runners, they can build up the necessary endurance if it is done gradually. In fact, the one thing you'll have to watch for is that the dog does not try to run too fast and burn himself out. It's a whole different thing for them to learn to lope along. Also, the pads on the dog's feet may be tender, so start out on soft surfaces, such as grass.

Whole books have been written on the subject of running with your dog, and you would do well to read at least one of them before you get started. Important health tips are included, as well as information on how to build up your dog's stamina.

Purina has, in recent years, sponsored the Purina Hi Pro K-9 Fun Run. The specifics of the runs vary from city to city, but they generally feature a one-mile walk/run and, for the more physically fit, a two-mile run. If you and your Greyhound jog together regularly, you both would probably enjoy running with other people and dogs. And imagine your dog's surprise when he realizes that other dogs run, too!

RUN FOR CHARITY OR FUN

Many Greyhound adoption groups hold an annual run for adopters and their dogs. Some do it for the fun of it, while others do it to raise money for the rescue program. If the group you adopted your dog from doesn't have one, why don't you suggest it (and be the one to organize it)?

SHOWING YOUR GREYHOUND

Showing your Greyhound in American Kennel Club–sponsored shows is not an option for two reasons.

First, spayed or neutered dogs do not qualify, and your dog almost certainly has been altered. Remember, the purpose of showing is to breed the "best" dogs afterward, and breeding is not the idea behind adopting an ex-racing Greyhound.

Second, it is difficult, and in most cases, impossible, to get the registration papers for your dog. A dog without papers is also ineligible for showing.

There is an alternative, however. My group, Make Peace With Animals, has an annual event called the Greyhound Homecoming, a picnic attended by all of the Greyhounds, accompanied by their new families, that were adopted through us. One popular event during the day is the Dogs of Distinction ceremony. "Judges" award certificates for such categories as Longest Tail, Biggest Ears, Whitest Teeth, Oldest and so on. The idea, of course, is that all the dogs have something unique to offer and that each one is a winner. And that, too, is the idea behind adopting. Other adoption groups hold similar gatherings, and yours can too.

OBEDIENCE TRIALS

Don't be upset about your dog's truncated show career — cheer up! He can still compete in obedience classes. For that you must get an AKC Indefinite Listing Privilege number and proof that the dog has been spayed or neutered.

If you decide to pursue obedience, get a good trainer who is kind and who understands retired racers. Greyhounds are a quick study, and generally do quite well in obedience.

VISIT THE ELDERLY OR INFIRM

You can have fun with your ex-racer and do a good deed at the same time by taking him to visit hospitals and nursing homes. Many institutions recognize the therapeutic value of such visits. My own adoption group, Make Peace With Animals, has a

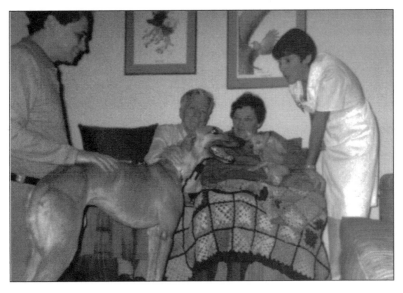

Elderly shut-ins enjoy a visit from
Alexandra, a Greyhound, and Paco, a Chihuahua.

program called AmbassaDogs®, and we have discovered that, because of their docile nature, Greyhounds are ideal visitors. Two requirements, of course, are that the dogs be housebroken and obedience trained. Some facilities also require that dogs pass the AKC-administered Canine Good Citizen program. It is a very moving experience to sit quietly with an older person or someone who is ill, watch them pet a Greyhound and see the joy on their face. Again, if your adoption group doesn't have such a program, why not initiate one?

THE GREYHOUND HALL OF FAME

In Abilene, Kansas (also the home of the National Greyhound Association), there is a museum dedicated to the Greyhound. Any dyed-in-the-wool Greyhound enthusiast must consider this the equivalent of Mecca. While the emphasis is on racing, there are interesting educational exhibits about the history of the breed, as well as examples of art depicting the Greyhound. A side treat is meeting Derby, a retired racer who has found a second career as the official mascot of the museum.

The Greyhound Hall of Fame in Abilene, Kansas.
(Photo: Greyhound Hall of Fame)

ADOPTING MORE GREYHOUNDS

If you're like most people who adopt a Greyhound, you'll soon find that one is not enough. I'm sure your adoption group will be happy to accommodate you. Before you proceed, keep in mind the original traits you were looking for (cat-safe, good with kids and so on) as well as how many dogs you can reasonably afford in terms of time and money. Also remember that two dogs can become competitive over food, toys and attention. Feed them separately, take away toys when you're not around to supervise and make sure you give your existing Greyhound an extra amount of affection once the new dog arrives. One way you might find the right second dog for you is by asking your adoption group if you can foster a dog for them. By having a trial run, you'll know for sure if the new Greyhound will fit into your existing household.

SPREAD THE WORD ABOUT ADOPTION

Finally, here is another way to have fun and get more people interested in adopting Greyhounds. You will discover very soon after adopting that people will constantly stop you and your dog on the street and say one of two things: "What kind of dog is that? He's so beautiful!" or "Is that one of those racing Greyhounds I've heard about?"

What you can do is this: always be prepared with either a descriptive brochure about adopting or with cards giving the name and number of someone who can be contacted for adoption information. You'll be amazed at the number of people who have always wanted an ex-racing Greyhound but didn't know where to get one. Although it is a lot of fun to sing your dog's praises, Greyhounds, being the wonderful dogs that they are, make even better spokes-dogs than you could ever be. And remember, for every card or brochure you hand out, there is the possibility that you will have helped a dog in dire need find the loving home he deserves.

Appendix One

Other Sighthounds

Afghan Hound

Basenji

Borzoi

Ibizan Hound

Irish Wolfhound

Italian Greyhound

Pharaoh Hound

Rhodesian Ridgeback

Saluki

Scottish Deerhound

Whippet

Appendix Two

The Greyhound's Anatomy

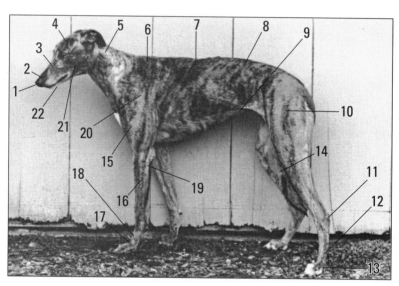

1. Nose	9. Loin	17. Pastern or
2. Muzzle	10. Rump	metacarpus
3. Stop	11. Hock	18. Wrist or carpus
4. Apex of skull	12. Pastern	19. Elbow
5. Neck	13. Toes	20. Shoulder
6. Withers	14. Stifle or knee	21. Cheek
7. Back	15. Chest	22. Flew
8. Hip	16. Forearm	

Appendix Three

Veterinary Information

HOW TO INTERPRET
TICK TITER RESULTS

Every testing laboratory has its own baseline titers and uses its own code for blood-work results. Here is how to decipher the code of the Protatek Reference Lab in Chandler, Arizona, a leader in tick testing for Greyhounds. If you use another laboratory, the relative values will be the same but the absolute values may be different.

LYME (B. BURGDORFERI)

    Baseline 1:640 — very weak exposure

    Results up to 1:10,000 — retest in 6 to 8 weeks

    Results over 1:10,000 — treat with doxycycline

BABESIA (BABESIA CANIS)

    Baseline 1:40 — possible weak exposure, not significant

    Results 1:80 to 1:320 — significant for exposure/infection; recommend CBC, serum chemistry; check for borderline anemia or elevated liver enzymes

Results under 1:640 with good blood-work — recheck in a year

Results over 1:640 — treat with Imidocarb injection

ROCKY MOUNTAIN SPOTTED FEVER (R. RICKETTSII)

Baseline 1:40 — very weak exposure

Results 1:80 to 1:320 — mild exposure in past, recheck in a month

Results greater than 1:640 — treat with doxycycline

EHRLICHIA (EHRLICHIA CANIS)

Baseline 1:10 up to 1:40 — not significant

1:80 or greater — treat with doxycycline or tetracycline for two to three weeks

Please note: With Ehrlichia, the longer the dog has been infected, the higher the titer. A longer course of antibiotics may be necessary.

RECOMMENDED ANESTHESIA PROTOCOLS FOR SIGHTHOUNDS

Courtesy of Nicole Timbrook, RVT, Surgery and Anesthesia Department Supervisor, The Veterinary Referral Centre/Cardiopet in Little Falls, New Jersey.

FOR SHORT, NON-INVASIVE PROCEDURES (SUTURE/ STAPLE REMOVAL, X-RAYS, BANDAGE PLACEMENT/ REMOVAL, ETC.)

Propofol to effect: Draw up 3 to 4 mg/kg of Propofol and administer *slowly* via IV with a butterfly catheter until the desired anesthetic plane is reached. Then give in small increments, 0.25 to 0.5 mg/kg, until conclusion of the procedure. Additional Propofol may be required for longer procedures, and an adjunct drug such as Diazepam (Valium) can be given at 0.15 to 0.25 mg/kg IV to increase the effectiveness of the Propofol while decreasing the total amount needed for the procedure.

Please note: Short-acting alpha-2 agonists such as medetomidine (Dormitor) are *not* recommended for Greyhounds due to the breed's low resting heart rate and their lean body mass. Use of alpha-2 agonists may cause dysrhythmias.

FOR SURGICAL PROCEDURES OR ANY PROCEDURES REQUIRING GENERAL ANESTHESIA

PREOPERATIVE MEDICATION

Drug	Concentration	Dose	Route
Glycopyrrolate	0.2 mg/ml	0.005–0.01 mg/kg	IM
Acepromazine*	1 mg/ml	0.01–0.02 mg/kg	IM
Hydromorphone (Dilaudid)	2 mg/ml	0.07–0.1 mg/kg	IM

*Use dilute Acepromazine for accurate dosing

Note: All three medications can be drawn up into the same syringe and administered IM.

INDUCTION

Drug	Concentration	Dose	Route
Diazepam (Valium)*	5 mg/ml	0.15–0.25 mg/kg	IV
Propofol	10 mg/ml	1.0–3.0 mg/kg	IV

*Diazepam should be administered just prior to starting the Propofol, which should be infused slowly and then discontinued once the patient has reached an adequate depth that permits intubation with an endotracheal tube.

MAINTAINING ANESTHESIA

Inhalant anesthetics isoflurane and sevoflurane are generally safe for use in all sighthound breeds.*

*See warnings by Dr. Alan Klide concerning malignant hyperthermia on page 119.

FLUID THERAPY

During general anesthesia for invasive procedures, intravenous fluids are recommended at a surgical rate of 10ml/kg/hr. If the patient has evidence of cardiac or respiratory disease, the fluid rate should be decreased to 3 to 7 ml/kg/hr, depending on the severity of the disease.

POSTOPERATIVE ANALGESIA

Drug	Concentration	Dose	Route
Hydromorphone (Dilaudid) OR	2 mg/ml	0.07–0.1 mg/kg	IM or slow IV
Buprenorphine (Buprenex)	0.3 mg/ml	0.01 mg/kg	IM

Note: Disassociative agents (ketamine, telazol) are contraindicated for use in Greyhounds because of the likelihood that they will cause exaggerated emergence delirium (e.g., thrashing, swallowing their tongue and screaming) upon recovery from short procedures. When used for longer procedures (those lasting longer than 60 minutes), and when used in combination with sedative agents, recovery is generally uneventful.

VETERINARY REFERENCES

STUDIES

"Thyroid Function Testing in Greyhounds," by Kathy R. Gaughan, DVM and David Bruyette, DVM, *American Journal of Veterinary Medicine*, Vol. 62, No. 7, July 2001.

"Thyroid Function of the Racing Greyhound," by M. Bloomberg, DVM, MS, University of Florida, School of Veterinary Medicine, 1987.

"Hematologic and Serum Biochemical Reference Values in Retired Greyhounds," by J. Steiss, DVM, W. Brewer, DVM, E. Welles, DVM, J. Wright, DVM, *Compendium on Continuing Education*, March, 2000.

ARTICLES

"Orthopedic Foundation of America Thyroid Certification," by Teri Dickinson, DVM, www.italiangreyhound.org/ofathyroid.html, Copyright 1996–2003, The Italian Greyhound Club of America.

"Medical and Laboratory Idiosyncracies of Greyhounds," *Antech Diagnostics Newsletter*, Lake Success, NY, March, 2002.

"What's In Those Blood Tests?" by Suzanne Stack, DVM, www. arizonaadoptagreyhound.org/blood_tests.html.

BOOK

Care of the Racing Greyhound: A Guide for Trainers, Breeders and Veterinarians, by Linda L. Blythe, DVM, PhD, James R. Gannon, BVSc, FACVSc, A. Morrie Craig, PhD, American Greyhound Council, Inc, 1994.

Appendix Four

Adoption Groups

The following is a list of all known Greyhound adoption groups worldwide. **Inclusion does not signify endorsement.** It is strongly recommended that you interview potential groups to find the right one for you. (List courtesy of The Greyhound Project.)

UNITED STATES

ALABAMA

*Greyhound Pets of America/
Northern Alabama*
954 Shady Grove Rd.
Adamsville, AL 35005
205-833-6654, 800-366-1472
gpabham@bellsouth.net

Greyhound Retired Racers
17107 Andrews St.
Athens, AL 35614
256-233-1288, 877-477-4381
grr@adopt-a-greyhound.org

Retired Racers Adoption Center
c/o Mobile Greyhound Park,
P.O. Box 43
Theodore, AL 36590
334-653-4900, 334-653-5000
mgp7101@bellsouth.net
www.mobilegreyhoundpark.com

ARIZONA

*FastDogs-FastFriends Greyhound
Rescue and Adoption*
13018 N. 59th Dr.
Glendale, AZ 85304
623-773-0534, 602-622-0991
info@fastdogs-fastfriends.com
www.fastdogs-fastfriends.com

*Greyhound Pets of America/
Arizona*
P.O. Box 2365
Glendale, AZ 85311-2365
800-366-1472
rory.s.goree@worldnet.att.net

Arizona Adopt a Greyhound Inc.
P.O. Box 63033
Phoenix, AZ 85082
602-971-6935

*Greyhound Rescue in the
Red Rocks (GRRR)*
Att: Ann Sakowicz
P.O. Box 357
Sedona, AZ 86336
520-204-1235
annpru@cybertrails.com

Greyhound Adoption League
3288 SkyHawk Dr.
Sierra Vista, AZ 85650-6623
520-378-1763
azgreyhounds@earthlink.net
www.azgreyhounds.com

Arizona Greyhound Rescue
8987 E. Tanque Verde Rd.
Suite 309/153
Tucson, AZ 85749
520-886-7411
director@azgreyhoundrescue.org
www.azgreyhoundrescue.org

Greyhound Adoption League
4310 S. Calico Lane
Tucson, AZ 85735
520-578-2792, 520-322-9095
azgreyhounds@earthlink.net
www.azgreyhounds.com

ARKANSAS

*Mid-South Greyhound Adoption
Option*
P.O. Box 2088
West Memphis, AR 72301
870-735-7317
greyhounds@clunet.com

CALIFORNIA

Retired Racers Inc.
6027 Valley Sage Rd.
Acton, CA 93510
661-269-2544
greymail@retiredracers.com
www.retiredracers.com

Amazing Greys~Retired Racers
PMB A227, 1145 2nd St.
Brentwood, CA 94513
209-835-9780, 925-513-0983
jtbar@aol.com

*Northern California Greyhound
Adoption Program (NCGAP)*
3044 Portillo Court
Cameron Park, CA 95682
530-672-2258, 925-935-7658
ncgap@aol.com
www.ncgap.com

Operation Greyhound
273 Chicory Lane
El Cajon, CA 92021
619-588-6611
operationgreyhound@cox.net
www.operationgreyhound.com

*Greyhound Adoption Center —
Orange County, Los Angeles,
San Bernardino & Riverside Areas*
4905 Basswood Lane
Irvine, CA 92612
949-786-0835
talldog@cox.net
www.greyhoundog.org

Hemopet/Pet Life-line
11330 Markton Dr.
Gordon Grove, CA 92841
714-891-2022

Needle Nose Crew
4857 Royce Rd.
Irvine, CA 92612
949-552-5661
information@needlenosecrew.org
www.needlenosecrew.org

Canine Causes
P.O. Box 7205
Laguna Niguel, CA 92677
949-457-1566
CanineCauses@cox.net
www.caninecauses.com

*Greyhound Pets of America/
Orange County & Greater
Los Angeles*
1210 N. Cypress St.
La Habra Heights, CA
90631-3018
562-694-3519, 562-693-3450
gpa.ocgla@verizon.net
www.fastfriends.org

Greyhound Adoption Center
P.O. Box 2433
LaMesa, CA 91943-2433
877-GR8T-DOG, 619-443-0940
greyhound@greyhoundog.org
www.greyhoundog.org

Greyhound Connection
P.O. Box 84797
San Diego, CA 92138-4797
619-286-4739
www.greyhoundconnection.org

*Greyhound Adoption Center —
Central & Northern
California & Bay Area*
3914 N. Del Rey Ave.
Sanger, CA 93657
559-298-2029
Grey4Us@aol.com
www.greyhoundog.org

*Southern California
Greyhound Adoption League —
San Diego County*
P.O. Box 1337
Spring Valley, CA 91979
858-486-5532

*Greyhound Pets of America/
Greyhound Adoption
California/NC*
1582 Wright Ave.
Sunnyvale, CA 94087
408-749-0899, 209-836-9196
sassae@att.net
www.greyhoundadoption
california.com

Golden State Greyhound Adoption
PMB 182,
2977 Ygnacio Valley Rd.
Walnut Creek, CA 94598
925-946-0426
4greyts@ca.astound.net
www.goldengreyhounds.com

COLORADO

Rocky Mountain Greyhound Adoption Inc.
2824 Cordry Court
Boulder, CO 80303
303-449-3718, 720-685-6987
Altadena10@aol.com
www.rmga.org

Recycled Racers Inc.
6200 Dahlia St.
Commerce City, CO 80022
303-227-4737, 303-288-1591
greyadopt1@aol.com
www.recycledracers.org

Colorado Greyhound Companions Inc.
P.O. Box 271789
Fort Collins, CO 80527
970-207-1064, 970-226-8632
gcg@webaccess.net
www.webaccess.net/~cgc

Friends of Retired Greyhounds (FOR Greyhounds)
P.O. Box 273365
Fort Collins, CO 80527-3365
970-834-2125, 303-477-8615
ajafek@hotmail.com
www.FORgreyhounds.org

Greyhounds First Inc.
5633 State Highway 12
La Veta, CO 81055-9769
303-755-4140
milehirltr@aol.com

Colorado Greyhound Adoption Inc.
P.O. Box 2404
Littleton, CO 80161-2404
303-283-2799
Janets@nvmedia.com
www.greyhoundadoption.com

CONNECTICUT

REGAP of Connecticut Inc.
P.O. Box 76
Bethany, CT 06524
203-393-1673

Shoreline Star Greyhound Park
255 Kossuth St.
Bridgeport, CT 06608
800-GO-DOG-GO, ext. 342,
203-576-1976, ext. 342
Crys1982@aol.com
www.pupswithoutpartners.org

We Adopt Greyhounds (WAG) Inc.
P.O. Box 519
Cheshire, CT 06410
Audice@aol.com
www.wag-inc.org

Plainfield Pets
137 Lathrop Rd.
Plainfield, CT 06374
860-564-3391

Racing Owners Assisting Racers (ROAR)
P.O. Box 31
Plainfield, CT 06374
860-564-0000

FLORIDA

Hollydogs Greyhound Sanctuary
11405 Longfellow Lane
Bonita Springs, FL 34135
941-948-PETS, 877-EXRACER
Hollydogs@aol.com
www.Hollydogs.org

*Greyhound Rescue and Adoptions
of Tampa Bay (GREAT) Inc.*
P.O. Box 3007
Brandon, FL 33509-3007
813-971-4732
www.Great-Greyhound.org

Joey's Greyhound Friends Inc.
P.O. Box 101327
Cape Coral, FL 33910
239-549-7693, 239-542-7716
joeysGHfriends@aol.com
www.joeysgreyhoundfriends.org

*Humane Society of
North Pinellas Inc.*
3040 State Road 590
Clearwater, FL 33759
727-797-7722, 727-797-7206
hsnp@aol.com

Pet Greyhounds Inc.
215 Edgewood Ave.
Crescent City, FL 32112
904-698-2920

*Greyhound Pets of America/
Daytona Beach Chapter*
2201 W. International Speedway
Blvd.
Daytona Beach, FL 32114
904-239-3647
BMi1406548@aol.com

*Debby's Dogs — New Beginnings
Greyhound Adoption*
4400 SW 95 Ave.
Davie, FL 33328
954-370-6556
topdog@debbysdogs.org
www.debbysdogs.org

Ebro Greyhounds As Pets
6558 Dog Track Rd.
Ebro, FL 32437
850-234-3943, ext. 112,
850-535-4048, ext. 112

Friends of Greyhounds Inc.
P.O. Box 100894
Fort Lauderdale, FL 33310-0894
954-578-0072
Michelle@friendsofgreyhounds.org
www.Friendsofgreyhounds.org

Second Chance for Greyhounds
1434 Claret Court
Fort Myers, FL 33919-3458
941-947-2365

Hollydogs Greyhound Adoption
1600 S. Dixie Highway
Hollywood, FL 33020
954-925-7758
hollydogs1@aol.com
www.hollydogs.org

*The National Greyhound
Foundation Inc.*
P.O. Box 929
Homosassa, FL 34487
352-628-2281
Topdog@4greyhounds.org
www.4greyhounds.org

*Greyhounds As Pets of Northeast
Florida*
P.O. Box 54249
Jacksonville, FL 32245
904-389-2934
904-646-0001, ext. 1092
gap@jaxkennel.com
www.jaxkennel.com

*Greyhound Pets of America/
Greater Orlando*
1260 S. County Road 427
Longwood, FL 32750
407-332-4754
gpago@greyhoundpetsorlando.org
www.greyhoundpetsorlando.org

Greyhound Pets of America/Largo
P.O. Box 8071
Madeira Beach, FL 33738-8071
727-595-7852
lstolliver@aol.com
www.greyhoundpets.com

*Greyhound Pets of America/
Central Florida*
3525 Manassas Ave.
Melbourne, FL 32934
321-242-9010
cfgpa.digital.net

Homeward Bound Greyhounds
6017 Pine Ridge Rd., #261
Naples, FL 34119-3956
941-353-7335, 941-353-7335
homewardbndgreys@cs.com

*Brandywine Downs Greyhound
Adoption*
1200 NW 73rd Terrace
Ocala, FL 34482
352-873-2727
Ghound23@aol.com

Adopt a Florida Greyhound Inc.
P.O. Box 1833
Palm City, FL 34991
561-349-3647

Valentine Adoption
1134 Harrison Ave.
Panama City, FL 32401
850-265-6667, 850-747-1020
Zoi2go@aol.com

EscaRosa Greyhound Adoption
9200 Magnolia Springs Rd.
Pensacola, FL 32526
850-944-2033
escarosagreys@aol.com
members.aol.com/escarosagreys/

*Greyhound Pets of
America/Emerald Coast*
P.O. Box 30426
Pensacola, FL 32503-1426
850-968-2010
Annbo47@cs.com, Ann@
gpaec.com, info@gpaec.com
www.gpaec.com

Humane Society of
Seminole County
2800 County Home Rd.
Sanford, FL 32773
407-323-8685

Racing Dog Rescue Project Inc.
P.O. Box 18153
Sarasota, FL 34276
941-379-3278, 941-915-6585
RDRP@comcast.net
www.rdrp-greyhound.org

The Greyhound Gang
of Florida
P.O. Box 1885
Seffner, FL 33583
813-684-4804
greyhoundgangfl.hotmail.com
www.greyhoundgangfl.org

Greyhound Adoptions of
Florida Inc.
8405 SE 128 Lane
Summerfield, FL 34491
352-347-9622
greys100@mpinet.net
www.ahome4greys.org

Greyhound Adoption League of
South Florida Inc.
4128 Hibiscus Circle
West Palm Beach, FL 33409
561-615-0818

Greyhound Pets of America/
Florida Southeast Coast
7047 Belevedere Rd.
West Palm Beach, FL 33411-3303
800-336-1472, 561-478-3006
gpa@gate.net
www.greyhoundpetsfl.org

GEORGIA

Greyhounds Galore
889 Luke Smith Rd.
Macon, GA 31211
912-742-0474
jbrantley@redi.net
www.mylink.net/~petadopt

Greyt Friends Inc.
2969 Gant Quarters Dr.
Marietta, GA 30068
770-971-8788, 706-682-5848
dee@greytfriends.org
www.greytfriends.org

Greyhound Pets of America/
Atlanta-Southeastern
Greyhound Adoption
364 Country Club Rd.
Newnan, GA 30263-6221
770-GREYPET
SEAdopt@greyhoundAdoption.org
www.greyhoundadoption.org

Adopt a Greyhound Atlanta
4815 Annistown Rd.
Stone Mountain, GA 30087
770-469-9533
adopt@greyhounds2.org
www.greyhounds2.org

National Sighthound Rescue &
Adoption Inc.
2399 Fredonia Rd.
Thomasville, GA 31757
229-226-7632
NSRA@compuserve.com

The Sanctuary
144 S. Campbell Ave.,
P.O. Box 2948
Tybee Island, GA 31328
912-786-7666, 912-484-7666
Gryhndluvr@aol.com

Friends of Greyhounds as Pets
P.O. Box 266, 302 E. 4th St.
Woodbine, GA 31569
912-576-5232
dkgrey@eagnet.com
www.friendsofgap.org

IDAHO

Greyhound Rescue of Idaho
1770 W. State St., #PMB 119
Boise, ID 83702
208-377-0645, 208-377-8057

Sighthound Adoption and
Fostering Center
5407 Saddle St.
Boise, ID 83709
208-362-1147
sighthound@earthlink.net
www.easy-finder.com

Greyhound Pets Inc.
1900 Millview
Coeur d'Alene, ID 83814
208-765-3115, 800-228-7794
www.GreyhoundPetsInc.org

ILLINOIS

National REGAP Network
P.O. Box 1327
Barrington, IL 60011-1327
800-379-2341 in Illinois,
847-622-5440 outside Illinois
adopt@regap.org
www.regap.org

REGAP of Illinois Inc./
Chicago Regap
7725 Forest Preserve
Chicago, IL 60634-6036
773-625-5545, 708-349-8448
regap1@juno.com
communities.msn.com/
REGAPofIllinois

Greyhound Guardians Inc.
13432 W. Arabian Dr.
Lockport, IL 60441
708-301-0780
www.greyhoundguardians.org

REGAP of Illinois Inc./
Chicago Regap
P.O. Box 128
Orland Park, IL 60462
708-349-8448, 773-625-5545
kmansmom92@aol.com
communities.msn.com/
REGAPofIllinois

*Central Illinois Greyhound
Adoption*
2208 Sierra Dr.
Pekin, IL 61554
309-346-0570
chelsea@mtco.com
www.geocities.com/ciga2001/
homepage.html

Peoria Greyhound Adoption Inc.
P.O. Box 1253
Peoria, IL 61654
309-688-0021, 309-923-8941
PeoriaGreyhound@hotmail.com
www.greyhound-adoption.org

*Quad Cities Greyhound
Adoption*
5103 11th St.
Rock Island, IL 61201
309-793-4578, 563-326-3336
gcgr8thnds@yahoo.com
www.qcgreyhoundadoption.org

Greyhound Aid
P.O. Box 562
Streamwood, IL 60107

*Midwest Greyhound
Adoption Inc.*
P.O. Box 338
Sugar Grove, IL 60554
630-466-4022, 630-851-3402
Adoptmga@aol.com
www.midwestgreyhound.org

Greyhounds Only
743 Landon Ave.
Winthrop Harbor, IL 60096
847-731-2511,
773-297-GREY (4739)
GOInc@aol.com
www.GreyhoundsOnly.com

Greyhound Pet Connection
P.O. Box 458
Woodstock, IL 60098
815-568-8403
Fastdogs@bigfoot.com

INDIANA

*USA Defenders of Greyhounds Inc.
(USA DOG)*
P.O. Box 1256
Carmel, IN 46082
317-244-0113, 317-867-1704
www.usadog.org

Greyhound Guardians Inc.
3224 Rustic Lane
Crown Point, IN 46307
219-661-0350, 219-763-1893
ggpres@msn.com,
Ggpaper@Yahoo.com
www.greyhoundguardians.org

Greyt Rescues
P.O. Box 127
Dayton, IN 47947-0127
765-447-9110
dtnice@netusa1.net
www.netusa1.net/~dtnice/
greyt.html

Central Indiana REGAP Inc.
7945 E. 100 N.
Greenfield, IN 46140-9457
317-462-0019
rjregap@aol.com

*Greyhound Pets of America/
Indianapolis*
6010 Hayford Way
Indianapolis, IN 46254
317-293-2502, 317-782-3901
roberts359@aol.com
www.gpaindy.org

*Greyhound Pets of
America/Indiana Chapter*
4414 S. 100 E.
Lafayette, IN 47909
765-471-1832
indiana.greyhounds@verizon.net
www.gpaindiana.org

*American Greyhound/
Great Lakes Inc.*
P.O. Box 30
Westville, IN 46391
219-926-1577
american_greyhound@
hotmail.com
www.americangrey.org

IOWA

Heartland Greyhound Adoption
P.O. Box 342
Bondurant, IA 50035
515-967-6564, 515-963-9317
meyergl@hotmail.com
www.heartlandgreyhound
adoption.org

*Dubuque Greyhound Park
Adoption Program*
P.O. Box 3190
Dubuque, IA 52004
800-373-3647
adopt@dgpc.com
www.dgpc.com/greyhounddata.
htm

*Bluffs Run Greyhound
Adoption Program*
P.O. Box 396
Pacific Junction, IA 51561
712-622-8334
lovely@netins.net
www.bluffsdogs.com

*Greyhound Pets of
America/Midwest*
2397 Utah Ave.
Thor, IA 50591
515-378-3183
Lovely@netins.net

KANSAS

Pups Without Partners
P.O. Box 12036
Kansas City, KS 66112
913-596-5955
Adopt@pups-without-
partners.org
www.pups-without-partners.org

Houndhaven
1208 High St.
Leavenworth, KS 66048
913-772-7777, 913-469-4037
Houndhaven@aol.com

*Greyhound Pets of America/
Kansas*
323 2400 Ave.
Solomon, KS 67480
785-655-2208
tlckansas@yahoo.com
www.tlcgreyhoundadoption.com

WGP Adoption Center
1500 E. 77th N., P.O. Box 277
Valley Center, KS 67147
316-755-4000

*Race the Wind Greyhound
Adoption Inc.*
1500 E. 77th St. N.
Valley Center, KS 67147
316-755-4000
greydogs@swbell.net
www.racethewind.org

KENTUCKY

*Greyhound Pets of America/
Southern Ohio Valley*
P.O. Box 72237
Louisville, KY 40272-0237
502-995-3767, 502-935-3974
GFord33@aol.com
www.canineworld.com/gpa-sov

*Greyhound Rescue and Adoption
of Kentucky Inc.*
P.O. Box 99913
Louisville, KY 40269
877-943-8364
adopt@adoptagreyhound.com
www.adoptagreyhound.com

*Mid-South Greyhound Rescue
Adoption Option Inc.*
16901 Ash Hill Dr.
Louisville, KY 40245
502-253-0883, 502-253-0884
dmkee@msn.com

Greyhounds of Shamrock
P.O. Box 991216
Louisville, KY 40269-1216
502-241-3140
questions@greyhoundsof
shamrock.org
www.greyhoundsofshamrock.org

Homes for Greyhounds Inc.
688 Walker Park Rd.
Richmond, KY 40475
859-623-6045
Hosea@iname.com
www.planetcraft.com/greyhound

LOUISIANA

*Greyhound Pets of
America/Louisiana*
106 Pineoak Dr.
Covington, LA 70433
504-893-0966 Judi
225-924-4556 Flo
FloRink@aol.com
www.greyhoundpets.org

MAINE

*Maine Greyhound
Placement Service*
P.O. Box 682
Bridgton, ME 04009
207-846-4707, 207-647-8944
Grayhoun@megalink.net
www.greyhoundplacement.com

MARYLAND

*Greyhound Pets of
America/Maryland*
P.O. Box 42103
Baltimore, MD 21284-2103
800-600-8607
gpa-md@adopt-a-greyhound.org
www.adopt-a-greyhound.org/
gpa-md.html

*Midlantic Greyhound
Adoption League Inc.*
P.O. Box 136
Clarksville, MD 21029
301-854-0816, 410-483-4697
MGAgreyhounds@aol.com,
jdillon@quan.lib.md.us
www.midlanticgreyhound.org

Greyhound Rescue Inc.
6397 Woodburn Ave.
Elkridge, MD 21075
410-796-2803, 703-323-0118
Greyhoundrescue@comcast.net
www.Greyrescue.org

A Greyhound's Wish Inc.
P.O. Box 603
Hanover, MD 21076
410-519-7300
agreyhoundswish@home.com
www.agreyhoundswish.org

Greyhound Welfare
P.O. Box 5273
Takoma Park, MD 20913
301-949-0615
kopalb@hotmail.com
www.greyhoundwelfare.org

The Ark for Greyhounds
11011 Old Frederick Rd.
Thurmont, MD 21788
301-898-7519

MASSACHUSETTS

Adopt a Greyhound, Inc.
P.O. Box 512
Falmouth, MA 02541
508-540-0293, 508-540-0635
rbf682@aol.com
www.riverbendfarmkennels.com

Greyhound Friends West Inc.
5 Baldwin Hill Rd.
Great Barrington, MA 01230
914-454-6216, 914-868-1348
racing4hom@aol.com
www.jedco.com/greyfriends

Greyhound Friends Inc.
167 Saddle Hill Rd.
Hopkinton, MA 01748
508-435-5969
ghfriend@tiac.net
www.greyhound.org

GreysLand Greyhound Adoption
P.O. Box 358
Hopkinton, MA 01748
508-435-6023
adopt@greysland.org
www.greysland.org

Greyhound Rescue of
New England
P.O. Box 507
Mendon, MA 01756
508-478-1617
Adopt@greyhoundrescuene.org
www.greyhoundrescuene.org

Greyhound Pets of America-
Massachusetts
3 Smith St.
Middleboro, MA 02346
508-947-3654, 617-472-4055
happydog12@aol.com
www.greyhoundpets.org/chaplist

Off Track Pets
P.O. Box 172
Raynham, MA 02767
508-824-4071, ext. 412
general@rtgp.com
www.rtgp.com

Wonder Dogs
190 VFW Parkway
Revere, MA 02151
781-284-1300
www.wonderlandgreyhound.com

Northeast Animal Shelter
204 Highland Ave.
Salem, MA 01970
978-745-9888
www.northeastanimalshelter.org

Greyhound Adoption Service
16 Jak-Len Dr.
Salisbury, MA 01952
978-462-7973
Homes4grey@aol.com
members.aol.com/greycanine

Greyhound Options
12 Barnes St.
Ware, MA 01082
413-967-9088
Ckerr1@aol.com,
griehund@rcn.com
surf.to/greyhoundoptions

MICHIGAN

Michigan Greyhound Connection
P.O. Box 725384
Berkley, MI 48072-5384
800-398-4364
sbilsky@peoplepc.com
www.michgreys.com

Greyhound Angel Rescue
P.O. Box 1906
Dearborn, MI 48121
313-441-2804, 313-582-2374
cdrew31709@aol.com

Greyhound Rescue of Michigan
3623 Cedar Lake Rd.
Howell, MI 48843-9666
517-552-0118, 313-359-0857
Nancy@greyhoundrescuemi.org
www.greyhoundrescuemi.org

GreyHeart Greyhound Rescue &
Adoption of Michigan Inc.
33748 Trillium Court
Livonia, MI 48150
586-406-4531, 313-937-0472
dazygrey@aol.com
www.greyheart.org

Greyhaven Greyhound Rescue
797 W. Pickard Rd.
Mount Pleasant, MI 48858
989-772-5097
Tariat@aol.com

Second Chance for
Greyhounds of Michigan
P.O. Box 2438
Portage, MI 49081
616-349-5104
joanne.connors@scfg.org
www.scfg.org

Michigan REGAP
P.O. Box 806131
St. Clair Shores, MI 48081
1-800-GoHound, 810-773-7991
rgpleslie@mindspring.com
www.retiredgreyhounds.com

Hav-A-Heart Greyhound Rescue
and Adoption
877 E. McGregor Rd.
St. Louis, MI 48880
517-681-2028

Greyhound Pets of America/
Michigan
25420 Mintdale Rd.
Sturgis, MI 49091
616-887-3440, 616-651-7395
rperry@voyager.net
www.gpamichigan.org

TLC/MI Greyhound Adoption
1274 138th Ave.
Wayland, MI 48348
616-792-2144
greyhndhotel@triton.net
www.tlcmi.org

GreytHounds of Eastern Michigan
P.O. Box 194
Wayne, MI 48184
877-GEM-DOGS
gemboard@gemgreyhounds.org
www.gemgreyhounds.org

Renewed Life for Greyhounds Inc.
16245 Van Buren St.
West Olive, MI 49460
616-786-3430, 616-335-8725
staff@renewedlife.org
www.renewedlife.org

MINNESOTA

Northwoods REGAP
7355 Pelton Rd.
Britt, MN 55710
218-741-5723, 218-780-0457
paws_up_north@yahoo.com

*Northern Lights Greyhound
Adoption*
11247 Foley Blvd.
Coon Rapids, MN 55448
763-754-9754, 763-755-3595
Guber2nac@aol.com
www.nlga-mn.org

*Greyhound Pets of
America/Minnesota*
P.O. Box 49183
Minneapolis, MN 55449
763-785-4000
Sistertex@softworksinc.net
www.gpa.mn.org

Rochester REGAP
1235 Center St.
Rochester, MN 55902
507-287-0478
www.rochesterregap.org

Twin City REGAP
P.O. Box 131963
St. Paul, MN 55113
651-487-1076
tcregap@yahoo.com

MISSISSIPPI

*North Mississippi
Greyhound Adoption*
132 RD 2256
Tupelo, MS 38824
601-869-7389
kimginn@ebicom.net
www.ebicom.net/~kimginn

Jane and Dennis Harmon
P.O. Box 52
Columbus, MS 39703
800-748-9673, 622-329-3949
dharmon@stargtr.net

MISSOURI

*Greyhound Pet Adoptions
of Kansas City*
7309 NW 79th St.
Kansas City, MO 64152-2150
816-584-8506
gentlehugs@juno.com

Kansas City REGAP
7400 E. 102nd St.
Kansas City, MO 64134
816-763-3333
Cboliver@qni.com
www.kcregap.org

*Greyhound Companions
of Missouri*
P.O. Box 19902
St. Louis, MO 63144
314-839-1525
rrc@tseinc.com
www.gcmo.org

Rescued Racers
10929 St. Henry Lane
St. Louis, MO 63074
314-423-4126, 314-921-7379
gdoglady@yahoo.com
www.rescuedracers.com

St. Louis REGAP
P.O. Box 25383
St. Louis, MO 63125
314-894-0834, 314-544-5729
stlregap@hotmail.com
www.regap.com

*Greyhound Pets of America/
Springfield*
P.O. Box 3693
Springfield, MO 65808
417-883-8156, 417-887-6439
agreyhound@mindspring.com
www.gpamo.com

MONTANA

*Greyhound Pets of America/
Rocky Mountain*
364 Elk Trail
Whitefish, MT 59937-8433
406-862-3656
Sherig@digisys.net

NEVADA

*Greyhound Adoption and
Rescue/Nevada*
416 Sunburst Dr.
Henderson, NV 89015-8334
702-565-8892, 702-338-2407
greyhoundsnv@aol.com
www.greytrescue.org

Greyhounds as Pets Inc.
939 Santa Ynez Ave.
Henderson, NV 89015

*Greyhound Adoption Center —
Las Vegas, Nevada Area*
7008 Picaroon Lane
Las Vegas, NV 89145
702-304-0079, 877-GR8TDOG
stealthn@infi.net
www.greyhoundog.org

*Greyhound Pets of
America/Southern Nevada*
P.O. Box 71803
Las Vegas, NV 89170-1803
702-392-5822, 800-366-1482
info@lasvegasgreyhounds.org
www.LasVegasGreyhounds.org

Nevada Greyhounds Unlimited
P.O. Box 210
Silver Springs, NV 89429
775-557-2414, 775-246-9006
Houndluv@aol.com
www.nevadagreyhounds.org

NEW HAMPSHIRE

Tailwind Greyhound
Adoption Program
368 North West Rd.
Canterbury, NH 03224
603-783-5988
TailwindAdoption@aol.com

Greyhound Pets of America/
New Hampshire
P.O. Box 778
Concord, NH 03302-0778
603-225-2175

Hinsdale Greyhound Park
Route 119 Brattleboro Rd.
Hinsdale, NH 03451
603-336-5382, 800-648-7225
www.hinsdalegreyhound.com

Greyhound Placement Service
P.O. Box 58
New Boston, NH 03070
603-497-2148
gpstopdog@attbi.com
www.gpstopdog.org

Retired Greyhounds As Pets
(REGAP)
Seabrook Greyhound Park
P.O. Box 1861
Seabrook, NH 03874
603-474-3065, ext. 7
makepeace@thepipeline.net
www.abra.petfinder.com

Fast Friends
P.O. Box 674
West Swanzey, NH 03469-0674
603-357-7376
fastfriends@msn.com
www.helpinggreyhounds.org

NEW JERSEY

Greyhound Rescue Inc.
P.O. Box 365
Fanwood, NJ 07023
908-754-8342

New Jersey Greyhound Adoption
Program Inc.
723 County Road 625
Hampton, NJ 08827
908-832-9678
www.njgreyhounds.org

Greyhound Friends
of New Jersey Inc.
170 Township Line Rd.
Hillsborough, NJ 08844
908-874-0508
yml96@aol.com
www.greyhoundfriendsnj.org

Hound Haven Inc.
P.O. Box 45
New Vernon, NJ 07976
973-455-0202
www.Hound-Haven.com

Make Peace With Animals, Inc. —
New Jersey
105 Robbinsville-Edinburg Rd.
Robbinsville, NJ 08691
609-448-1742, 215-862-0605
Jofother@aol.com
www.makepeacewithanimals.org

NEW MEXICO

New Mexico Greyhound
Connection
7220 Cascada Rd. NW
Albuquerque, NM 87114
505-897-0427, 505-453-4627 (cell)
JBeck72726@aol.com

A Place for Us Greyhound Rescue
194-A County Line Rd.
Edgewood, NM 87015
505-873-1729, 505-286-4413
elaur@twrol.com
www.greyhound-data.com/apfuga

NEW YORK

Greyhound Rescue Adoption Team
(GReAT)
P.O. Box 196
Buffalo, NY 14207
716-839-4275
adoption@greathounds.org
www.greathounds.org

Syracuse Area Greyhound Adoption
7198 Klock Rd.
Canastota, NY 13032
315-697-3819
www.syracuseareagreyhound
adoption.org

Buffalo Greyhound Adoption Inc.
P.O. Box 1096
Cheektowaga, NY 14225
716-873-1165
omfp@b-g-a.org
www.b-g-a.org

Greyhound Rescue of
New York Inc.
P.O. Box 1527
Clifton, NY 12065
webmaster@greyhoundrescue.com
www.greyhoundrescue.com

Simply GH's Ltd.
74 Rensselaer Ave.
Cohoes, NY 12047

Greyhound Rescue &
Rehabilitation (G.R.R.)
P.O. Box 572
Cross River, NY 10518
914-763-2221
greytest1@aol.com
www.greyhoundrescuerehab.org

Greyhounds as Companions
1770 Delaware Turnpike
Delmar, NY 12054
518-768-2579, 518-452-4422

Long Island Greyhound Transfer
Inc. (L.I.G.H.T.)
89 Pengon Circle
East Meadow, NY 11554
516-735-6073
ligreyhound@hotmail.com
www.ligreyhound.org

Grateful Greyhounds
20 Penny Lane
Levittown, NY 11756
516-735-5070
greyhoundsavior@aol.com
http://gratefulgreyhoundsny.com

*Greyhound Adoption of
Central New York*
305 Third St.
Liverpool, NY 13088
315-457-7989, 315-682-5810
jonnagrey@aol.com

*Greyhound Acres Rescue
and Adoption*
9181 Red Hill Rd.
New Hartford, NY 13413
315-737-0424, 315-737-0537
gryhndacre@aol.com
www.greyhound-acres.8m.com

ASPCA
424 E. 92nd St.
New York, NY 10128
212-876-7700, ext. 4421
jacques@aspca.org
www.ASPCA.org

Make Peace With Animals Inc.
529 Centre Island Rd.
Oyster Bay LI, NY 11771
516-922-1852, 516-741-5958
Greyzoom@optonline.net
www.makepeacewithanimals.org

Greyhound Outreach
1789 Lamson Rd.
Phoenix, NY 13135
315-678-2173
greyhoundoutreach@yahoo.com

Fast Track Greyhound Adoptions
588 W. Mountain Rd.
Queensbury, NY 12804
518-793-9463, 518-793-4200
sueblair1967@hotmail.com
www.petfinder.org/shelters/
NY141.html

*Greyhound Pets of America/
Western New York*
P.O. Box 22715
Rochester, NY 14692-2715
888-322-7801, 716-288-0758
Joangpa@eznet.net
www.gpa.org

*Homestretch Greyhound
Adoptions Inc.*
317 Perry St.
Schenectady, NY 12306
518-372-7024, 518-584-3780
lebugli@crd.ge.com
www.members.aol.com/
sportum10

NORTH CAROLINA

*Greyhaven Senior and Special
Needs Greyhounds*
5530 Old Noble Rd.
Cedar Grove, NC 27231
919-732-6110, 919-260-1504
greysincharge@yahoo.com

*Greyhound Friends of
North Carolina*
P.O. Box 19194
Greensboro, NC 27419-9194
336-643-0233, 336-601-7810
gfncadpt@BellSouth.net
www.greyhoundfriends.com

Project Racing Home
P.O. Box 8434
Greensboro, NC 27419
336-852-9444, 336-728-2501
projectracinghome@yahoo.com
www.project-racing-home.com

Sanford Animal Hospital
P.O. Box 2157
Sanford, NC 27330

*Circle of Friends Greyhound
Adoption and Sighthound
Rescue Inc.*
1058 N. Main St.
Walnut Cove, NC 27052
336-591-8867, 336-747-5291
JTDearmin@aol.com
www.circleoffriendsgreyhounds.
net

Homes for Hounds
5120 Davis Rd.
Waxhaw, NC 28173
Homes4hounds@aol.com

Greyhounds of Distinction
P.O. Box 5692
Wilmington, NC 28403
910-251-1414
jnewton1@ec.rr.com

OHIO

Lucky Greyhounds
2239 A St., Route 131
Batavia, OH 45103

Ohio Friends of Greyhounds
3921 Logan NW
Canton, OH 44709
330-492-3859

*Ohio Greyhound
Gathering Adoption*
3570 Shepler Church SW
Canton, OH 44706
330-484-1720, 330-875-4702
jlammmm@sssnet.com

Greyhound Adoption of Ohio
7122 County Lane
Chagrin Falls, OH 44023
440-543-6256, 800-269-1148
www.GreyhoundadoptionofOH.
org

*Team Greyhounds Adoption
of Ohio Inc./Cinncinati*
1757 Acreview Dr.
Cincinnati, OH 45240
513-385-3751, 513-742-9452
ladyanne@ladyanne.com
www.teamgreyhound.com

Golden Years Senior Greyhounds
P.O. Box 24310
Cleveland, OH 44124
440-516-0874
Ohiogreyhounds@yahoo.com
www.geocities.com/ohio
greyhounds/seniors.html

Love at First Sight
Greyhound Adoption
270 E. Main St.
Cortland, OH 44410
330-637-5228
bads1line@acninc.net

Lake Erie Greyhound Rescue
278 N. Broadway
Geneva, OH 44041
440-466-1347
greyhound@ncweb.com
greyhound.marinar.com

Rebound Greyhounds
7036 Pine Grove Dr.
Hubbard, Ohio, 44425
330-534-8649, 330-720-8624 (cell)
AdoptAGreyhound@aol.com
www.reboundgreyhounds.org

Pioneer City Friends of
Greyhounds
130 Rauch Dr.
Marietta, OH 45750
740-374-4533
valliejo@charter.net
www.pioneercitygreyhounds.org

Greyhound Pets of America/
Wheeling Downs
P.O. Box 391
Martins Ferry, OH 43935
304-232-4492, 800-366-1472
gpawdoh@aol.com

Ohio Greyhound Placement
8379 Martingale Lane
Russell, OH 44072
440-338-1744
ohiogreys@aol.com
www.geocitites.com/Heartland/
Hills/7235/

Team Greyhound Adoption
of Ohio Inc.
4413 County Road 2
Swanton, OH 43558
419-825-3476
Nancy@teamgreyhound.com
www.teamgreyhound.com

OKLAHOMA

GPA Central Oklahoma Hounds
of Heartland
3136 NW 22nd
Oklahoma City, OK 73107
405-948-8801, 405-340-8209
home4hounds@cox.net,
Gr8uro@aol.com
www.greyhoundpetsok.org

Greyhound Pets of
America/Oklahoma
1775 E. 59th St.
Tulsa, OK 74105
918-712-1775, 918-744-1810
gpaok@home.com
www.gpaok.com

Halfway Home Greyhounds
6321 S. Richmond
Tulsa, OK 74136
918-492-8077
greytmama@aol.com
www.halfwayhomegreyhounds.
com

OREGON

Multnomah Greyhound Park
P.O. Box 9
Fairview, OR 97204
503-677-7700

*Greyhound Pets of
America/Northwest*
P.O. Box 6524
Portland, OR 97228
800-366-1472
greyhnds@open.org
www.gpa-nw.org

Homes for Hounds
5081 SW Pacific Highway
Waldport, OR 97394
541-563-3467
HomesForHoundsh4h@
hotmail.com
www.homesforhounds1.
homestead.com

PENNSYLVANIA

*Monica's Heart Greyhound
Adoption*
1408 E. Hamilton Lane
Altoona, PA 16602
814-942-1906, 814-942-3145
houndmom@charter.net

Personalized Greyhounds Inc.
128 Old Ford Dr.
Camp Hill, PA 17011
717-761-3317
pginc@webtv.net
www.pgreys.org

*Grey-Save of Northwestern
Pennsylvania*
P.O. Box 8612
Erie, PA 16505-9998
814-796-4504, 814-825-7825
greysave@aol.com
members.aol.com/greysave/
Index.html

*National Greyhound
Adoption Program of Northwest
Pennsylvania*
P.O. Box 10002
Erie, PA 16514
814-456-4969, 814-899-8261
houndad@aol.com

*Rainbow's End
Greyhound Rescue*
RR2, Box 457B
Harvey's Lake, PA 18618
570-639-2612, 570-822-9815
dakc@ptd.net

Make Peace With Animals Inc.
P.O. Box 488
New Hope, PA 18938
215-862-0605, 610-760-8562
makepeacewithanimals@
makepeacewithanimals.org
www.makepeacewithanimals.org

*National Greyhound
Adoption Program Inc.*
4701 Bath St.
Philadelphia, PA 19137
215-331-7981
ngap@ix.netcom.com
www.ngap.org

Nittany Greyhounds
142 Greyhound Lane
Port Matilda, PA 16870
814-692-7614
nittanygreys@aol.com
www.nittanygreyhounds.org

*First State Greyhound
Rescue Inc.*
2110 Newark Rd.
West Grove, PA 19390
610-869-5941, 610-987-6859,
215-443-7065
exracergrey@hotmail.com
www.firstgreys.org

Going Home Greyhounds
P.O. Box 513
Wexford, PA 15090
724-935-6298
nah@nauticom.net

Linda Ann's Greyhound Adoption
1531 Allen St.
Allentown, PA 18102
610-437-3188
JLAgreys@webtv.net

RHODE ISLAND

*Lincoln Greyhound Adoption
Program*
1600 Louisquisset Park
Lincoln, RI 02865
401-781-6231, 401-724-7979
www.LincolnParkRI.com

SOUTH CAROLINA

*Greyhound Crossroads
Adoption Service*
Intersection of Highway 34 and 36,
P.O. Box 6117
Chappells, SC 29037
864-995-3112, 864-995-3000
GreyCrazy@aol.com
members.carol.net/greycrazy

Carolina Greyhound Connection
P.O. Box 965
Drayton, SC 29333
864-582-4824
carolinaghconnection@prodigy.net
pages.prodigy.net/
carolinaghconnection

*Greyhound Pets of America/South
Carolina Greyhound Adoptions*
416 W. Main St.
Lexington, SC 29072
803-749-3174, 803-359-4371
greyhound@sc.rr.com
www.GPA-SC.com

GreytHound Love
213 Meetze Ave.
Lexington, SC 29072
803-957-3866, 803-748-7395
jhorton8@sc.rr.com

Greyhounds & Love
5030 White City Park Rd.
Anderson, SC 29625
864-224-5921
greyhoundsandlov@aol.com
www.greyhoundandlove.org

TENNESSEE

*Greyhound Rescue Foundation
of Tennessee*
P.O. Box 53623
Knoxville, TN 37950
865-690-6009, 865-690-0009
greyhoundrescuefoundation
oftn@yahoo.com
www.greyhoundrescue.org

*Greyhound Pets of
America/Tennessee*
P.O. Box 23231
Knoxville, TN 37933-1231
865-671-2749
tmarshal@conc.tds.net

*Tennessee Alliance for
Greyhounds Inc. (TAG)*
P.O. Box 362
Loudon, TN 37774
865-458-6710, 865-458-6650
Taghounds@aol.com

*Greyhound Pets of
America/Nashville*
1016 Draughon Ave.
Nashville, TN 37204
615-460-7259, 615-418-7216
greyhoundpetsnashville@
hotmail.com
www.greyhoundpets.org/chaplist

TEXAS

*Greyhound Adoption League
of Texas Inc.*
P.O. Box 680
Addison, TX 75001-0680
972-503-GALT, 214-676-3544
info@greyhoundadoptiontx.org
www.greyhoundadoptiontx.org

Greyhound Rescue Austin
7611 Old Bee Cave Rd.
Austin, TX 78735
512-288-0068
starbright60@webtv.net
www.constant.com/~rory/gra

Greyhound Friends for Life
Route 1, Box 223A8
Canyon, TX 79015
806-499-3511

*Corpus Christi Greyhound Track
Adoption Program*
P.O. Box 9087
Corpus Christi, TX 78469

*Greyhound Rescue
Society of Texas Inc./
Greyhounds Unlimited*
P.O. Box 703967
Dallas, TX 75370-3967
972-503-Grey, 972-571-4526
info@greyhoundsunlimited.org
www.greyhoundsunlimited.org

Greyhound Adoption League
1820 Robert Wynn
El Paso, TX 79936
915-593-7006

*Greyhound Pets of
America/Central Texas*
P.O. Box 40086
Georgetown, TX 78628
512-454-9062, 512-930-9195
RFTrapp@aol.com

*Greyhound Pets of
America/Houston*
P.O. Box 741176
Houston, TX 77274
713-667-3804, 713-866-4466

Gulf Greyhound Adoption
P.O. Box 488
LaMarque, TX 77568
800-275-2946, 281-481-0351

*Greyhound Pets of America/
Texas — San Antonio*
P.O. Box 702016
San Antonio, TX 78270-2016
210-722-1920
greythound@gpasa.org
www.gpasa.org

*Heart of Texas Greyhound
Adoption Inc.*
24430 Camp Site
San Antonio, TX 78264
210-621-0123, 210-509-8224
contact@heartoftexas
greyhounds.com
www.heartoftexasgreyhounds.com

Hill Country Greyhound Adoption
P.O. Box 543
Seguin, TX 78156
830-303-2229
hcga@swbell.net

*Sakkara Greyhounds/
North Texas*
1320 Azalea Lane
Sulphur Springs, TX 75482
903-885-6671, 903-885-8875
tkhyde@neto.com

UTAH

Second Chance Greyhounds
11757 S. 7th E.
Draper, UT 84020
801-571-2439
jburt@softcom.net

Greyhound Gang
P.O. Box 274
Kanab, UT 84741
435-644-2903
claudia@greyhoundgang.org
www.greyhoundgang.org

Greyhound Rescue and Adoption,
Utah Chapter
P.O. Box 12492
Ogden, UT 84412-2492
801-737-4289
greyraceno@yahoo.com
www.ladyofgreys.org

VERMONT

Greyhound Rescue of Vermont
P.O. Box 1632
Williston, VT 05495
802-878-4844, 802-482-2673
rundog@globalnetisp.net
www.vtgreys.org

VIRGINIA

Greyt Expectations
Greyhound Rescue
20545 Chingville Rd.
Leonardtown, VA 20650
301-994-2414, 804-330-0259
greytexpectationsrescue@
yahoo.com
www.geocities.com/greyt
expectationsrescue

Virginia Greyhound Adoption
P.O. Box 710912
Oak Hill, VA 20171
703-437-1044 Northern Virginia,
804-457-9509 Richmond
adopt@virginiagreyhounds.org
www.virginiagreyhounds.org

Greyhound Pets of America/
Virginia-Richmond
P.O. Box 70811
Richmond, VA 23255-0811
804-527-3584

NGAP of Virginia
636 Piney Point Rd.
Virginia Beach, VA 23452
757-486-7956, 757-479-4133
gryhound@infi.net
www.ngap.org/NGAP_Va

Greyhound Pets of America/
Northern Virginia
P.O. Box 6037
Woodbridge, VA 22195
800-366-1472, 703-538-4926
psfol@aol.com
www.gpa-nova.org

WASHINGTON

Greyhound Pets of America/
Puget Sound
2310 Hoyt Ave.
Everett, WA 98201
425-339-9230, 425-348-9822
eld@serv.net
www.psgreyhounds.org

Greyhound Pets Inc.
5514 22nd Ave. SE
Lacey, WA 98503
360-459-1586, 425-788-3835

Greyhound Pets of America/
Emerald Pacific
9428 108th St. SW
Lakewood, WA 98498-3006
253-589-1532
greyhound@worknet.att.net

Greyhound Pets of America/
Inland Empire
4910 N. Karen Rd.
Otis Orchards, WA 99027
509-927-8002
www.greyhoundpets.org/
emerald-pacific.html

Royal Hounds
P.O. Box 731391
Puyallup, WA 98374
253-841-3005, 206-935-6399
royalhounds@dog.com
www.royalhounds.org

Greyhound Pets Inc.
342 NW 76th St.
Seattle, WA 98117
206-781-1978, 206-714-0852
Leslie@speakeasy.org
www.greyhoundpetsinc.org

WEST VIRGINIA

West Virginia Greyhound
Adoptions
P.O. Box 202
Charlton Heights, WV 25040
304-744-9012, 304-779-9122
Janscwv@aol.com

Tri-state Greyhound Adoption
Program & Rescue Center
P.O. Box 7118
Cross Lanes, WV 25356
776-1000, ext. 270, 776-8530
Cheryl34@intelos.net

Greyhounds Adopting Families
Prestige Park, Suite 500-B
Hurricane, WV 25526-8430
304-757-0071
adopt@countryroadskennel.com
www.countryroadskennel.com

Greyhound Pets of America/
Wheeling Downs
1 S. Stone St.
Wheeling, WV 26003
304-232-5050, ext. 1899,
800-366-1472
gpawheeling@aol.com
www.wheelingdowns.com

WISCONSIN

Retired Greyhound Athletes Inc.
3811 Cripple Creek Dr.
Appleton, WI 54913
920-749-0133, 920-336-1580
info@retiredgreyhound
athletes.org
www.retiredgreyhoundathletes.org

Geneva Lakes Kennel Club
Adoption Center
P.O. Box 650
Delavan, WI 53115
800-477-4552, ext. 501,
262-728-8000, ext. 501

Dairyland Greyhound Park
Adoption Center
5522 104th Ave.
Kenosha, WI 53140
262-612-8256, 800-233-3357
www.Dairylandgreyhoundpark.com

Wisconsin REGAP
4100 Easter Rd.
LaCrosse, WI 54601
608-787-6280, 608-781-4014
foxs@email.western.tec.wi.us.

Greyhound Pets of America/
Wisconsin
P.O. Box 2115
Madison, WI 53701-2115
414-299-9473
www.gpawisconsin.org

INTERNATIONAL

AUSTRALIA

Greyhound Adoption Program
(Queensland)
P.O. Box 250
Albion, Queensland,
Australia, 4010
61-7-3262-7800

Greyhound Adoption
Program (NSW) Inc.
P.O. Box 24
Belrose West, NSW,
Australia, 2085
02-9452 3446, 02-9451 0323
d.wigney@vetp.usyd.edu.au

Greyhound Adoption Program
(Western Australia)
P.O. Box 6
Cannington, WA,
Australia, 6987
61-8-9458-4600,
61-040-888-3669
kvernon@greyhoundswa.com.au
www.grehoundswa

Greyhound Pets of Queensland
10 Morrison Court
Cedar Grove, Queensland,
Australia, 4285
07554 33229, 073 2089465
jaydee@fan.net.au

Greyhound Adoption Program
(South Australia)
P.O. Box 2352
Regency Park, SA,
Australia, 5942
61-8-8268-1211

Sandown Veterinary Clinic
P.O. Box 13
Springvale, Victoria,
Australia, 3161
03-9547-6666

BELGIUM

Greyhounds in Nood Belgium/
Mireille Broeders
Jan.Breydelstraat 32-34
9000 Gent, Belgium
0032.9.282.60.65
m.broeders.greyhounds.in.nood.
be@skynet.be
users.skynet.be/greyhounds.in.
nood.belgium/

CANADA

Greyhound Rescue Quebec
432 Hampton Court
Dollard des Ormeaux, Quebec,
Canada, H9G 1L3
514-624-6335, 514-620-0038
sherlessmith@yahoo.ca
www.greyhoundrescue.bigstep.com

Greyhounds of Georgetown
31 Chaplin Crescent
Georgetown, Ontario,
Canada, L5G 5Y4
905-873-2943

Northwest Canadian
Greyhound League
P.O. Box 23365
Grande Prairie, Alberta,
Canada, T8V 7G7
780-402-1997, 780-505-2112
koenenb@telusplanet.net
www.telusplanet.net/
public/koenenb

Greyhounds Circle of Friends
c/o Joanne and Rodney Hopkins
109 E. 19th St.
Hamilton, Ontario,
Canada, L9A 4R9
905-388-5361
greyhounds@bigwave.ca

Greyhound Lovers of
Hamilton Wentworth
3600 Golf Club Rd., RR #1
Hannon, Ontario,
Canada, L0R 1P0
905-692-5790, 905-648-1119
glohw@glohw.on.ca
www.glohw.on.ca

*Greyhound Pets of
Atlantic Canada*
7 Lake Front Dr.
Lake Echo, Nova Scotia,
Canada, B3E 1C7
902-829-3306
Greyhnd@ns.sympatico.ca
www.gpac.ca

*Greyhound Relocation and
Adoption, Canada*
RR 1, 283250 Daniel Rd.
Mt. Elgin, Ontario,
Canada, N0J IN0
519-425-7822
GRACanada@aol.com
http://GRA.RTS.ca

Niagara Greyhound Adoption Inc.
5740 Heritage Dr.
Niagara Falls, Ontario,
Canada, L2J 3J8
905-354-9488, 905-563-1666
nga@xracer.ca, www.xracer.ca

*Adopt a Greyhound of
Central Canada Inc.*
RR #3
North Gower, Ontario,
Canada, K0A 2T0
613-489-0654
inof@adopt-a-greyhound.com
www.adopt-a-greyhound.com

*Greyhounds in Need of
Adoption Inc.*
656 Steele St.
Port Colborne, Ontario,
Canada, L3K 4Y9
905-835-2078, 416-429-5274
Katie@inter-pc.com
www.saveagrey.com

Greyhound Pets Inc.
97–52349, RR #222
Sherwood Park, Alberta,
Canada, T8C 1A3
780-922-0545, 780-466-4237
itsfr@telusplanet.net
www.greyhoundpetsinc.org

ENGLAND

Greyhound Rescue
Derwent View
Brackenholme Nr. Selby,
N. Yorkshire, UK, YO8 7EL
44 1757 638889

Evesham Greyhound Rescue
7 Hinton Rd.
Childswick, Broadway, UK,
WR12 7HY
44 1386 853971

Greyhounds in Need
5 Greenways
Egham, Surrey, UK, TW20 9PA
44 1784 436845
Anne@greyhoundsinneed.
f9.co.uk
www.greyhoundrescue.co.uk

*Walthamstow Homefinding
Scheme*
Whittingham Kennels
No. 6 Cleverhambury, Galley
Hill, Waltham Abbey
Essex, UK, EN9 2BL
0020 8444 9649
greyhounds@ntlworld.com
homepage.ntlworld.com/
greyhounds

*Greyhound Rescue West
of England*
Highfield, Wombridge
Hereford, Herefordshire,
UK, HR2 9DD
07000 785092
beelineco@wyenet.co.uk
www.grwe.co.uk

Greyhounds in Notts
66 George St.
Hucknall, Nottingham,
UK, NG15 7DN
0115 9554453
Support@GreyhoundsInNotts.
co.uk
www.greyhoundsinnotts.co.uk

Greyhound Compassion
Dolphin Cottage, Longdrag Hill
Tiverton, Devon, UK, EX16 5AQ
44 1884 254727
sally.slater@greyhound.com
freeserve.co.uk
www.hounddog.org.uk

Retired Greyhound Trust (RGT)
149A Central Rd.
Worcester Park, Surrey,
UK, KT4 8DT
0208 335 3016, 01522 569825
retired@greyhounds.co.uk

GERMANY

Greyhound Rescue Deutschland
e.v., Schlossbachstrasse 20
Gaildorf, Germany, 74405
49 7971 3706, 49 7088 6882
greyhound-rescue@gmx.de

Greyhounds in Not
Holmgren & Gurner,
Hamburger Str. 4
Gross Niendorf, Germany, 23816
045 52 1533

HOLLAND

Greyhounds Rescue Holland
Hazendonk 20 – NL 5103 GH
Dongen, The Netherlands
0162-314396, 013-5365714
info@greyhoundsrescue.nl
www.greyhoundsrescue.nl

IRELAND

Kerry Greyhound Homefinders
Corrawoolia Glencuttane,
Lower Kilgobnet
Beaufort, Co. Kerry, Ireland
066-9762654
kerrygreyhound@eircom.net

SCOTLAND

Greyhound Awareness League
104 Stamperland Gardens
Glasgow, Scotland, UK, G76 8NR
0141-644-2570, 01899-308381
Denise@greyhoundawareness.
freeserve.co.uk
www.users.globalnet.co.uk/
~nenagh

SPAIN

SOS Galgos
calle Angel Guimera, n.17
Esplugues de Llobregat,
Barcelona, 08950
34 607 21 68 96, 34 93 372 56 85
sosgalgos@sosgalgos.com
www.sosgalgos.com

Amigos de los Galgos
C/. Ona 147 9o
Madrid, Spain, 28050
34 91 766 1258, 34 699736794
agnblanco@nodo50.org
www.nodo50.org/amigos
delosgalgos

Scooby Association
San Francisco 3
Medina del Campo, Spain, 47400
34 983 811087

SWITZERLAND

New Graceland
Allmendhusli, CH-6019
Sigigen, Switzerland, CH-6019
41 41 496 08 10, 41 52 319 17 04
mail@newgraceland.org
www.newgraceland.org

WALES

Greyhound Rescue Wales (CRW)
10 Penmaen Terrace
Mount Pleasant, Swansea,
Wales, UK, SA1 GHZ
44 1792 472196, 44 7071 88 10 68
grw@ukmax.co.uk
www.greyhound-rescue.demon.
co.uk

Greyhound Welfare
4 Caldey Place
Swansea, City and County of
Swansea, Wales, UK, SA5 5PN
44 0 1792 537540,
44 0 7967 813780
enquiries@greyhound_welfare.
org.uk
www.greyhound-welfare.org.uk

Appendix Five

Resources and Organizations

MAGAZINES

Celebrating Greyhounds Magazine

P.O. Box 358
Marblehead, MA 01945-0358
www.adopt-a-greyhound.org/cgmagazine

Quarterly magazine of The Greyhound Project, for new and seasoned owners and adopters.

The Greyhound Review
R.R. 3, Box 111B
Abilene, KS 67410
www.ngagreyhounds.com

Monthly magazine of the National Greyhound Association, covering the world of the racing Greyhound.

The Sighthound Review
10177 Blue River Hills Rd.
Manhattan, KS 66503
www.sighthoundreview.com

Bimonthly magazine covering the world of the show and coursing Greyhound and related sighthound breeds.

ACCESSORIES

Animal Magnetism
P.O. Box 101
Lambertville, NJ 08530
800-836-2546
www.AnimalMagnetism.com

Mail order Greyhound supplies, including specially made Greyhound winter coats, safety collars, coursing supplies, related books and gifts.

Doctors Foster and Smith
2253 Air Park Rd.
P.O. Box 100
Rhinelander, WI 54501-0100
800-826-7206
www.DrsFosterSmith.com

Extensive health-related supplies plus toys, chews and bedding.

Pet Edge
P.O. Box 128
Topsfield, MA 01983
800-738-3343
www.PetEdge.com

Mail order discounted dog crates and supplies.

ORGANIZATIONS

REGISTRIES

American Kennel Club
5580 Centerview Dr.

Raleigh, NC 27606
919-233-9767
www.akc.org

Greyhound Club of America
4280 Carpenteria Ave.
Carpenteria, CA 93013
805-684-4914
www.GreyhoundClubofAmerica.org

For AKC-registered Greyhounds.

Greyhound Hall of Fame
407 S. Buckeye
Abilene, KS 67410
785-263-3000
www.greyhoundhalloffame.com

National Greyhound Association
R.R. 3, Box 111B
Abilene, KS 67410
913-263-4660
www.NGAGreyhounds.com

Racing organization and registry.

COURSING/NOTRA RACING ASSOCIATIONS

AKC Lure Coursing
1235 Pine Grove Rd.
Hanover, PA 17331
717-632-6806

American Sighthound Field Association
1098 New Britain Rd.
Rocky Hill, CT 06067
860-563-0533
www.ASFA.org

Artificial lure coursing.

National Oval Track Racing Association (NOTRA)
13765 S. 1300

West Riverton, UT 84065
801-254-6817
www.NOTRA.org

RECOMMENDED READING

Care of the Racing Greyhound: A Guide for Trainers, Breeders and Veterinarians, by Drs. Linda Blythe, James Gannon and A. Morrie Craig, American Greyhound Council, 1994.

Childproofing Your Dog: A Complete Guide to Preparing Your Dog for the Children in Your Life, by Brian Kilcommons, Warner Books, 1994.

The Complete Book of Greyhounds, Edited by Julia Barnes, Howell Book House, 1996.

Dog Owner's Home Veterinary Handbook, by Drs. James M. Giffin and Liisa D. Carlson, Howell Book House, 2000.

The Dog Who Loved Too Much: Tales, Treatments, and the Psychology of Dogs, by Dr. Nicholas Dodman, Bantam Books, 1997.

GRRR! The Complete Guide to Understanding and Preventing Aggressive Behavior in Dogs, by Matthew Margolis and Mordecai Siegel, Little Brown, 2000.

Help For Your Shy Dog: Turning Your Terrified Dog Into a Terrific Pet, by Deborah Wood, Howell Book House, 1999.

Living With a Greyhound, Edited by Cynthia A. Branigan, Barrons, 2002.

The Loss of a Pet, by Dr. Wallace Sife, Howell Book House, 1998.

The Pill Book Guide to Medication for Your Dog and Cat, by Kate A.W. Roby and Lenny Southam, Bantam Books, 1998.

The Reign of the Greyhound: A Popular History of the Oldest Family of Dogs, by Cynthia A. Branigan, Howell Book House, 1997.

$\mathcal{I}$ndex

accessories, sources, 199
activities
    amateur racing, 148
    AmbassaDogs, 151–152
    artificial lure coursing, 141–147
    charity runs, 150
    dog shows, 150–151
    fun runs, 148–149
    jogging, 149–150
    obedience trials, 151
activity level, ownership, 20–22
adoption agency
    owner/dog matching, 32
    questions for, 29–30
adoption groups, 166–197
adoptions
    first impressions, 34–39
    information sharing, 153
    kennel selection process, 31–32
    multi-dog family, 56–59
    multiple, 153
    new-home introduction, 59–63
    reasons for returning dogs, 33
    record-keeping issues, 34–35
    retirement reasons, 36
    spay/neuter, 35–36
    versus foster home, 15
Advantage (imidacloprid), 112

advertisements, lost animal recovery, 136–137
Afghan Hounds, 2, 154
age, Greyhound selection, 22
age of owner, dog ownership, 13–14
aggression, reason for returning dog, 33
aggressiveness, Greyhound short-comings, 19, 25
ailments, adoption, 35, 36
amateur racing, 148
AmbassaDogs, 151–152
America, Greyhound history, 9
American Kennel Club (AKC)
    CGC (Canine Good Citizen), 152
    ILP (Indefinite Listing Privilege), 142
    lure coursing, 142–145
American Sighthound Field Association (ASFA), 142–145
anatomy, 160
anesthesia
    health concerns, 117–119
    malignant hyperthermia, 119
    protocols, 162–164
    reasons for avoiding, 38
    recovery enhancement, 119
    thiobarbiturates, 118–119
animal shelters, lost animal recovery, 136

apartments, dog ownership, 13
arthritis
    glucosamine/chondroitin, 86
    older dogs, 106
artificial lure coursing, 142–147
ASFA (American Sighthound Field
    Association), 142–145

babesiosis, 98–99, 161–162
baldness, racers, 36–37
basements, crate alternative, 65
Basenjis, 2, 155
bathrooms, crate alternative, 65
baths, 91–93
bedding
    children's intrusions, 75
    racing kennel layouts, 43–44
    swollen elbow concerns, 38
behavioral accidents, 125–126
behaviors
    reasons for returning dogs, 33
    Schoolteacher Syndrome,
        56–58
    separation anxiety, 55–59
bladder control, older dogs, 105
blood values, checking, 106
bone cancer (osteosarcoma),
    100–101
books, recommended, 201
Borzois, 2, 155
breeds, Greyhound history, 1–10
brood bitches, housing, 40
budgets, dog ownership, 14–15
Bulldog, Greyhound history, 8–9

canine cancer, lawn chemical, 120
Canine Good Citizen (CGC) pro-
    gram, AKC, 152
canine multivitamins, 86
canine toothbrush, 91

canned foods, raw meat
    substitute, 83
carbamates, insecticide, 110
Catal-Huyuk, Turkey, 2–3
cats, introduction to, 133–135
charity runs, dog/owner, 150
chemicals, 51, 120
children, 24, 33, 72–78, 136
choke collars, 130–131
coats
    bald bottom condition, 36–37
    color range, 28–29
    daily brushing, 93
    hound glove, 91–93
collars, 130–131, 144
colors, ownership questions, 28–29
combs, flea, 115
convalescing dogs, 87
coursing, 8–10, 142–147
coursing associations, 200
crates
    children's intrusion, 75
    housebreaking use, 123–124
    new-home introduction, 60–63
    purchasing, 64–65
    racing kennel layouts, 43–44
    secure environment, 78
    sizing, 65
    weaning process, 66

defecation
    behavioral accidents, 125–126
    housebreaking, 122–124
dewormers, 116
diet supplements, 86
dietary additives, 114–115
diseases, tick-borne, 97–99
dog proofing pools, 69–70
    ranges, 69
    windows, 69

INDEX

dog shows, Greyhound
    Homecoming, 150–151
dog sitters, 58–59
dog walkers, separation anxiety, 58
Dogs of Distinction, Greyhound
    Homecoming award, 150–151
doors, children's concerns, 76–77
Drontal Plus (praziquantel/
    pyrantel pamoate/febantel), 116

ear cleansing solution, 91
ears, older dog hearing, 104–105
Egypt, Greyhound history, 3–4
ehrlichiosis, 98–99, 162
elbows, swollen condition, 38
England, Greyhound history, 5–6,
    8–9
equipment
    artificial lure coursing, 141
    collars, 130–131
    dog ownership expense, 14
    harness, 132–133
    leashes, 131–132
    muzzles, 129–130
    new-home suggestions, 80–81
Europe, Greyhound history, 5–6
euthanization, older dogs, 107–108
exercise, 58, 61, 122–123
expenses, dog ownership, 14–15
eyes, 99–100, 104–105

fans, crate cooling uses, 65
feeding
    children's intrusion, 76
    homemade diets, 85
    new-home, 61, 86–88
    older dogs, 104
    racing kennel routine, 46
    serving suggestions, 83, 86–88
    twice-a-day importance, 83

females
    adoption, 35
    brood bitches, 40
    gender, 26–28
    kibble (dry food), 83
    size ranges, 25
    spaying, 88–89
fencing, 137–140
finances, dog ownership, 14–15
flea baths, 89
flea collars, 109–110
flea combs, 115
fleas, 89, 109–115
flexibility, owners, 40
flooring, smooth floors, 66–67
flyers, lost animal recovery, 136
food bowls, 87–88, 104
foods, 14, 58, 82–86
foster home, versus adoption, 15
Frontline (fipronil), 112
fun runs, 148–149

garages, crate alternative, 65
gates, children's concerns, 76–77
gender, ownership, 26–28
giardiasis, metronidazole, 116
grades, races, 50
Greece, Greyhound history, 4–5
Greyhound Hall of Fame, 152
Greyhound Homecoming, 150–151
grief recovery, 13, 107–108
grooming
    baths, 91–93
    bonding opportunity, 89
    flea baths, 89
    racing kennels, 44–45
    shampoos, 91, 93
    toenails, 67–68

handling, racing kennels, 44–45
harness, reasons for, 132–133

health concerns
    anesthesia, 117–119
    arthritis, 106
    behavioral accidents, 125–126
    dental care, 102–103
    flea collars, 109–110
    fleas, 111–113
    heartworms, 99
    insecticides, 110–111
    internal parasites, 116
    laryngeal paralysis, 101
    lawn chemicals, 120
    malignant hyperthermia, 119
    natural flea control, 114–115
    older dogs, 103–108
    osteosarcoma, 100–101
    pannus, 99–100
    PCV (packed cell volume), 96
    professional assistance, 93–94
    thyroid testing, 94–96
    tick-borne diseases, 97–99
    WBC (white blood count), 96
hearing, older dogs, 104–105
heartworms, SNAP test, 99
herbal preparations, fleas, 114
herbicides, canine cancer, 120
homemade diets, 85
hookworms, parasite control, 116
hospital visitations, 151–152
hound glove, grooming aid, 91–92
housebreaking, 122–124, 138
housing
    brood bitches, 40
    racing kennel layouts, 43–44
    space requirements, 16
hugging, children, 75
Huntmaster, 144
hypothyroidism, testing for, 94–96

Ibizan Hounds, 2, 156
identification tags, 80–81

IGR (insect growth regulator), 114
ILP (Indefinite Listing Privilege), 142, 151
in-ground pools, 69–70
injuries
    adoption, 35, 36
    lure coursing, 146–147
    racing hazard, 51–52
    windows, 68–69
inoculations, 14, 34–35
insecticides, 110–111
internal parasites, 116
intestinal worms, 116
invisible fencing, 137–138
Irish Wolfhounds, 2, 156
Italian Greyhounds, 2, 157
Italy, Greyhound history, 5

jogging, 149–150
joint problems, 86
judging
    artificial lure coursing, 143
    Greyhound Homecoming, 150–151

kennels, 31–32, 43–44
kibble (dry food), 14, 83–84
kitchens, crate alternative, 65

laryngeal paralysis (paralyzed larynx), 101
lawn chemicals, cancers, 120
layouts, racing kennels, 43–44
leashes, holding properly, 131–132
life span, Greyhounds, 22
lost animals, retrieving, 135–138
lure coursing, 8–10, 142–147
lure coursing associations, 200
Lure of Courser of Merit, 143
Lure Operator, lure coursing, 144
Lyme disease, 98–99, 161

magazines, 198
maiden race, 49–50
Make Peace With Animals, 150–152
males
    adoption, 36
    gender, 26–28
    kibble serving suggestions, 83
    neutering, 88–89
    size ranges, 25
marital relationships, 13
meats, E. coli bacteria concerns, 83
medications
    Anipryl, 113
    banned substances, 51
    chondroitin, 86
    Clindamycin, 98
    Clomicalm, 113
    Clomipramine, 113
    dog ownership expense, 14, 15
    doxycycline, 98
    Elavil, 113
    glucosamine, 86
    imidocarb diproprionate, 98–99
    metronidazole, 116
    NSAIDs, 106
    Phenylpropanolamine, 113
    separation anxiety, 59
    thiobarbiturates, 118–119
Middle Ages, history, 5–6
motivations, dog ownership, 11–12
music, 45–46, 58
muzzles
    animal introduction, 133–135
    racing kennel use, 43
    reasons for, 129–130

National Greyhound Association, Greyhound Hall of Fame, 152
neuter/spay, adoption, 35–36

NOTRA racing associations, 148, 200
nursing home visitations, 151–152

obedience training, 15, 127–129
obedience trials, 151
off-leash walking, 16–19
oils, diet guidelines, 85–86
older dogs, 104–105, 146–147
organizations, 199–200
organophosphates, concerns, 110
osteosarcoma (bone cancer), 100–101
Oval Racing Championship (ORC), 148
ownership
    adoption versus fostering, 15
    flexibility importance, 40
    Greyhound motivations, 15
    racing kennel responsibilities, 41–42
    reasons for, 11–12

packed cell volume (PCV), 96
pannus (Uberretter's Disease), 99–100
paralyzed larynx (laryngeal paralysis), 101
parasites, 14, 116
PCV (packed cell volume), 96
personality, desirable traits, 20, 38
Pharaoh Hounds, 2, 157
plastic crates, purchasing, 64–65
pools, dog proofing, 69–70
Precor, insect growth regulator, 114
Preventic (amitraz), 112–113
Program (lufenuron), 111
puppies, 48–49
pyrethrins, insecticides, 111

racers
  health issues, 36–38
  injury hazards, 51–52
  retirement reasons, 36
  set weight, 46
  track diet, 82
races
  amateur, 148
  banned substances, 51
  charity runs, 150
  fun runs, 148–149
  grades, 50
  Greyhound history, 10
  maiden race, 49–50
racing kennels
  background music, 45–46
  brood bitches, 40
  care/handling, 44–45
  daily routines, 43–44
  feeding, 46
  grooming, 44–45
  housing layouts, 43–44
  maiden race, 49–50
  muzzle use, 43
  owner responsibilities, 41–42
  puppy training, 48–49
  race grades, 50
  track diet, 82
  training, 46–49
  turnout pens, 43
ranges, dog proofing, 69
raw meats, E. coli bacteria, 83
records, adoption, 34–35
registries, 199–200
Renaissance, history, 6, 7
renters, dog ownership, 13
retirement, reasons for, 36
Revolution (selamectin), 112
rewards, lost animal recovery, 137

Rhodesian Ridgebacks, 2, 158
Rocky Mountain Spotted Fever,
  98–99, 162
Rome, Italy, Greyhound history, 5
runaways, retrieving, 135–138

Salukis, 2, 158
Scars, racers, 38
Schoolteacher Syndrome, 56–58
Scottish Deerhounds, 2, 159
separation anxiety, 55–59, 125–126
set weight, racing Greyhounds, 46
shampoos, dog-specific, 91, 93
sighthounds, 154–159
Sit command, obedience, 127–129
size, crate guidelines, 65
size, ownership consideration, 25
skin irritations, racers, 38
slip-leads, lure coursing, 144
small animals
  introduction to, 133–135
  ownership question, 22–23
  reasons for returning dogs, 33
smooth floors, navigation, 66–67
SNAP test, tick-borne disease, 99
socialability
  new dog introduction, 133
  ownership question, 22–23
  reason for returning dogs, 33
  small animals, 133–135
spay/neuter, adoption, 35–36
spikes, racing injury hazard, 52
spousal relationships, 13
squawkers, retrieval uses, 136
stainless steel bowls, 87–88
stairs, introduction, 70–72
stools, tapeworm recognition, 89
stoves, dog proofing, 69
stuffed toys, separation anxiety, 58

INDEX

supplements
    diet, 86
    natural flea control, 114–115
    thyroid, 94–95
swimming pools, 69–70
swollen elbows, racer's problem, 38

tapeworms, 89, 116
Task, cautions/concerns, 116
tattoos, lost animal recovery, 136
teeth, dental care, 102–103
territorial marking, 125
thyroids, testing, 94–96
Tick Arrest (amitraz), 112–113
tick-borne diseases, 97–99
ticks, 111–113, 115
tick titer results, 161–162
toenail trimmers, 67–68, 91
tooth scalers, 91, 103–103
toothpaste, 91
Torus, insect growth regulator, 114
toys, separation anxiety, 58
track diet, racing Greyhounds, 82
trainers, 41, 127
training
    behavioral accidents, 125–126
    housebreaking, 122–124
    in-house living, 121–122
    obedience, 126–129
    puppy introduction, 48–49
    racing kennels, 46–49
treats, 58, 73
trials, lure coursing, 142–145
Turkey, Greyhound history, 2–3
turnout pens, racing kennels, 43

Uberretter's Disease (pannus), 99–100
urination
    behavioral accidents, 125–126
    housebreaking, 122–124
    older dog bladder control, 105
    territorial marking, 125
urine analysis, racers, 51

vaccines, tick-born diseases, 97–99
vegetables, feeding guidelines, 84
veterinarians
    board-certified specialists, 78
    health information, 161–165
    initial health-check, 80
    lost animal recovery, 136
    selection guidelines, 78–80
    teeth cleaning, 102–103
veterinary fees, expense, 14
visitations, activity, 151–152
vitamins, food supplement, 86

Wales, Greyhound history, 6
walks, off-leash cautions, 16–19
watchdogs, Greyhounds, 19, 25
water, availability of, 88
weather, hazard, 139
weight, racing Greyhounds, 46
Whippets, 2, 159
whipworms, parasite control, 116
white blood count (WBC), 96
window shade cords, 69
windows, injury threat, 68–69
wire crates, 64–65

yards, never leave dog, 138–139